MALCOLM MUGGERIDGE

JESUS

THE MAN WHO LIVES

COLLINS, 8 GRAFTON STREET, LONDON

This book was designed and produced by
George Rainbird Limited, Marble Arch House,
44 Edgware Road, London W2

House Editor: John Hadfield
Picture Research: Penelope Miller
Designer: Margaret Thomas

© Malcolm Muggeridge 1975
First published in the United Kingdom in 1975 by
William Collins Sons & Company Limited.
This edition fiirst published in 1988.

ISBN 0 00 215384 X

Extracts taken from the Authorized Version of the Bible,
which is Crown Copyright, are reproduced with permission.

Illustration on half-title page:
And it came to pass in those days that
Jesus came from Nazareth of Galilee, and was
baptized of John in Jordan.
STAINED-GLASS WINDOW, NINETEENTH CENTURY

Frontispiece:
Then saith he to Thomas, Reach hither thy finger,
and behold my hands; and reach hither thy hand,
and thrust it into my side : and be not faithless, but believing.
STONE CARVING, LATE ELEVENTH CENTURY

CONTENTS

Page

FOR ALEC VIDLER
whose lifelong friendship and steady faith
have been a continuing source of strength
and inspiration

I write this book for love of your love
ST AUGUSTINE

PART I

Jesus Comes Into The World

> An idea becomes close to you only when you are aware of it
> in your soul, when in reading about it it seems to you that it
> has already occurred to you, that you know it and are simply
> recalling it. That's how it was when I read the Gospels. In
> the Gospels I discovered a new world: I had not supposed
> that there was such a depth of thought in them. Yet it all
> seemed so familiar; it seemed that I had known it all long
> ago, that I had only forgotten it.
> TOLSTOY, as recorded in Bulgakov's Diary, 18 April 1910

The coming of Jesus into the world is the most stupendous event in
human history. I say this as a Christian, recognizing, of course, that
the coming into the world of a Mohammed or a Buddha must seem,
in the eyes of a Moslem or Buddhist, of equal or even greater
significance, and that had I been born in Mecca or Bangkok instead
of in a south London suburb I might well have taken a different view.
Similarly, for that matter, the coming into the world of a Karl Marx
to a dedicated Marxist, or of a Mao Tse-tung to a dedicated Maoist.
As it is, belonging to a civilization which began with the birth of Jesus
some two thousand years ago, and reaching the conclusion – to me
inescapable – that whatever is truly admirable in the achievements of
the succeeding centuries, in art and literature, in music and architecture, in the quest for knowledge and in the pursuit of justice and
brotherliness in human relations, derives from that same event, I
cannot but see it as towering sublimely above all others. I have to add,
too, that over and above this, the revelation Jesus provided, in his
teaching, and in the drama of his life, death and Resurrection, of the
true purpose and destination of our earthly existence, seems to me,
even by comparison with other such revelations, to be of unique value
and everlasting validity. The fact that I happen to have come into
the world myself at a time when the revelation's impetus in history
gives every sign of being almost spent, and when Western Man is
increasingly inclined to reject and despise the inheritance it has
brought him, only serves to make me the more appreciative of it and

7

awed by it. In the same sort of way the last notes of the *Missa Solemnis* seem to contain the whole beauty of what has gone before, or the light of a June evening to hold all the glory of the day that is ending.

The story of how Jesus came into the world, what he said and did there, and how he left the world while still remaining in it, has, it is safe to say, been more told, mulled over, analysed and expounded and illustrated, than any other in human history. So many hands! So many and such diverse versions and interpretations! From the sweet rough dialogue of the Mystery plays and the haunting notes of Plainsong, to Renan's lush prose, Dickens's unctuous sentimentality and the fathomless inanity of D. H. Lawrence's *The Man Who Died*. Then on to the wasteland of Freudians, priests who have run out of their presbyteries and their monasteries, theologians celebrating the death of God, *exaltés* intoning LSD pieties, freaks and communards and clerical *Playboy* fans, all engaged in promoting by one means or another, consciously or unconsciously, what has become the great twentieth-century Jesus cult, with large and profitable affiliates in the entertainment industry.

Add to this the works, rows and rows of them, of actual or pseudo-scholarship, questing for the historical Jesus, the freedom-fighting Jesus, the erotic or phallic Jesus, the proletarian or revolutionary Jesus. Then, the new translations of the Bible, each, as it seems to me, stylistically speaking, more flat and unprofitable than the last, and all containing some element, greater or less, of what is called today 'revisionism', whereby Jesus's essential message is modified, if not drastically changed – as that his kingdom *is* of this world, that Man *can* live by bread alone and *must* lay up treasure on earth in the shape of an ever-increasing Gross National Product. Meaning is often the enemy of truth, and in retranslating more exactly the words of the Gospels what they say so splendidly can easily be lost. Asking God 'not to put us to the test', for instance, may well be a more accurate translation of Jesus's words in what has been called traditionally the Lord's Prayer, but asking Him to 'lead us not into temptation' echoes more poignantly and perfectly the longing of a sinful heart like mine. Future historians – assuming there are any interested in such matters – are likely to conclude that the more we knew about Jesus the less we knew him, and the more precisely his words were translated the less we understood or heeded them.

Amid this welter of speculation, elaboration and conjecture the four Gospels continue to provide the only basic texts; as it were, the inviolate genes of the Christian faith. We whose language is English may rejoice that in our Authorized Version we have a translation of incomparable artistry and luminosity; but in whatever language or version, it is the words of the Gospels as they have come down to us, with all their textual imperfections and historical and theological ambiguities, which have inspired many of the noblest lives and much of the greatest art and literature and music and architecture of our civilization. In the truest and most absolute sense, therefore, they may be called Holy Words, and without blasphemy attributed to God Himself. It is on behalf of these words that majestic buildings like Chartres Cathedral have been constructed, and that great saints like St Francis of Assisi have so joyously and wholeheartedly dedicated their lives to the service of God and their fellow men. To the greater glory of these words Bach composed, El Greco painted, St Augustine laboured at his *City of God* and Pascal at his *Pensées*; in them a Bunyan found his inspiration in describing a Pilgrim's journey through the wilderness of this world, and a Sir Thomas More comfort on his way to the scaffold. In our own time, they enabled a Dietrich Bonhoeffer to go serenely to his death, and a Simone Weil to derive solace and enlightenment from the affliction that was her lot. To what these words have brought us, and bring us, there is truly no end; if they have survived their commentators – especially their latter-day ones – then surely they must be considered immortal.

At the Hebrew University in Jerusalem some bits of the Old Testament that were discovered among the Dead Sea Scrolls have been mounted and put on display. I found these battered fragments of papyri, written in Jesus's time, deeply moving. It was just such writings as these which recorded and preserved the sayings and doings of Jesus for posterity. Who, looking at the Gospels when they existed in such a form – towards the end of the first century AD – could have foreseen all they were going to mean to generation after generation of Christians in alien faraway lands? That they would be chanted and intoned day after day, century after century, in towering cathedrals as in tiny conventicles. That they would be carried intrepidly to every corner of the earth, and in time bawled across the very stratosphere? That they would fill the minds and inflame the hearts of countless men and women, urging them on to fantastic achievements, carrying them on waves of ecstasy up to God's very throne? Barely comprehensible scribble, yes, but what scribble! Living words conveying a living faith; as it is put at the beginning of the Fourth Gospel, not just words, but *the* Word which became flesh and dwelt among us, full of grace and truth. Every writer, however lowly, must seek above all else to produce words that are alive, in the hope that they, too, may go on existing gracefully and truthfully, if only for a little while, for another day or week. How much more so when they relate to *the* Word which became flesh in the person of Jesus! Thus reflecting, I find myself recalling a prayer of St Augustine, himself one who knew from experience how desperately hard it is to use words, each, as he puts it, with a beginning and an ending, in such a way that they are like a steeple climbing into the sky. In the light of this arduous experience he prayed that he might be permitted to offer God 'the sacrifice of my thoughts and my tongue, but first give what I may offer you'. I echo the prayer.

It is rather more than a century since Ernest Renan's *Vie de Jésus* appeared. Its impact was sensational, and it ran through edition after edition; as did also the attacks upon it which soon followed in great profusion. What Renan did was, in effect, to drain the New Testament of its transcendental elements, making its central character, Jesus, an inspired teacher rather than part of the Christian Godhead, and his miracles an exercise in medical magic – as it might be, all done by pills. Renan's Jesus, that is to say, was a sort of virtuous and truthful Jean-Jacques Rousseau – if anyone as congenitally deceitful and untruthful as Rousseau can be considered as capable of such a transformation – who charmed and edified the simple people among whom he lived and taught. In this, Renan followed up, embellished and Gallicized the work of German theologians of his time; notably David Friedrich Strauss, whose *Das Leben Jesu* met with a similar explosive reception to Renan's *Vie de Jésus*. They have subsequently had innumerable imitators, whose humanization of Jesus has grown ever more audacious.

The new presentation of Jesus and his teaching which Renan did so much to popularize came just at the right time. Under the influence of science and the humanism it inculcated, many ostensible Christians were longing for the traditional Gospel narrative to be freed from what they considered to be its oppressive and suffocating load of dogma and hagiography. They wanted Jesus himself, as well as the Virgin Mary, the Apostles and the saints, to step out of their haloes and mingle as real people with ordinary men and women. It was precisely this that Renan achieved. He had been an ordinand himself, and then had drawn back from becoming a priest. So he understood perfectly, indeed shared, the current craving for a Christianity without tears; for an idyll rather than a drama, with a happy ending instead of that gaunt Cross rising so inexorably into the sky. At the same time, he was a Biblical scholar and gifted popular writer, who could tell his story elegantly, movingly, sincerely, and, above all, convincingly. It might almost be said that his *Vie de Jésus* amounted

to a first rough draft of *Jesus Christ Superstar* – something that, if he is now in a position to observe our contemporary scene, would scarcely be calculated to please him. Already, in his own lifetime, there were intimations of uneasiness about the position he had taken; '*au fond*', he wrote, '*je sens que ma vie est toujours gouvernée par une foi que je n'ai plus*'. It was a cry from the heart, touching, and even tragic, which described, not just his own plight, but that of many Christians who felt they had lost their faith. The children and even grandchildren of believers could, like Renan, coast along on the momentum of a faith they no longer had, but, as we have had occasion to realize all too clearly, the great-grandchildren find, when the momentum finally dies down, that they are living in a spiritual and moral vacuum; that the light which came into the world when Jesus was born, and that went on shining, however fitfully and sometimes murkily through the succeeding centuries, has gone out, leaving behind only darkness, and dreams that soon turn into nightmares.

Renan fabricated his idyll in the Holy Land itself, finding inspiration in the landscape Jesus had known, in the towns and villages by the Lake of Galilee he had frequented, and in the familiar scenes – sowers going forth to sow, shepherds tending their flocks, fishermen casting their nets – on which he had drawn for his parables and images. The simple Galileans of Jesus's time, whom Renan summons up to be the extras in his idyll, are portrayed as happy and pure of heart, removed geographically, and in every other way, from the depravity and sophistication of the Roman Empire in which they had been incorporated. They readily understand the entrancing words of the silver-tongued prophet who has come among them, and joyously accept the good tidings he brings. What a pleasing contrast he makes with another prophetic voice they have heard – that of John the Baptist crying in the wilderness; a strange, wild figure clothed in skins, and reputedly living on locusts and wild honey! Renan implies that John's influence on Jesus was positively harmful, in the sense that it turned him into ascetic courses alien to his own cheerful disposition, and even suggests that it was on the whole a deliverance for him when the Baptist's head was delivered on a charger to Herod's wife, and he disappeared from the scene, leaving Jesus free to follow his natural bent towards easy-going, happy living – providing additional wine when it ran out at a wedding feast, and preferring the company of women of easy virtue and other ostensible sinners to that of the more respectable and law-abiding among his followers and admirers. Here, Renan opened a rich vein which has been heavily worked, especially of late, to the point that Jesus is commonly believed today to have consorted largely with whores, drunkards and rogues of one sort and another. This impression has been so effectively conveyed that it requires quite an effort to recall how, according to the Gospels, Jesus spent most of his time in the company of his disciples, who, as far as we know, were impeccably respectable, while the households he chose to visit – for instance, the one at Bethany where Mary, Martha and Lazarus lived together – would seem to have been more in the style of a Jane Austen than of a John Gay or Henry Fielding.

On the shores of Renan's Lake of Galilee the sun always seems to be shining; in its waters fish are always abundant, and the very mules have mild oval eyes and long eyelashes. Contrasted with this delectable scene is Jerusalem, where the power of the Roman colonialists is flaunted, and their satrap, King Herod, has a palace, and where the collaborationist Jewish priests and officials maintain their own ecclesiastical and political establishment. Here, the winsome teacher of Renan's idyll who offers forgiveness to all who will follow him and accept his gospel of love, turns into a transcendental revolutionary, and as such is publicly executed. 'Rest now, amid thy glory, noble pioneer', Renan apostrophizes the crucified Jesus. 'Thou conqueror of death, take the sceptre of thy kingdom, into which for so many centuries thy worshippers shall follow thee by the highway which thou has opened up!' Such is the finale of the idyll Renan dreamed up, as, accompanied by his beloved sister, Henriette, he followed the course of Jesus's life in the actual places where it had been lived. Henriette died at Byblos, in Syria, while the work was still in progress, and, commemorating their companionship and all the help she gave him, he dedicated his *Vie de Jésus*, as he put it, to 'her pure soul reposing on God's bosom'. When he came to die himself some thirty years later – in 1892 – he had no such confidence in his own heavenly prospects. By that time what Pascal called the vast silences of eternity had come to fill him with dread and despair.

As it happens, I had occasion myself to follow the New Testament story in the Holy Land – in my case for the purpose of producing the commentary for three television programmes on the subject. This necessitated, like Renan, getting as near as possible to the actual scenes and places where the drama of Jesus's life had been enacted. For instance, the part of the River Jordan where John the Baptist preached and baptized; the road from Jerusalem to Jericho along which the traveller fell among thieves, to be succoured by the Good Samaritan; the hillside looking down on Jerusalem where Jesus wept to think of the misfortunes which lay ahead for the city; the wilderness where he encountered the Devil. All these places remain vividly in my mind; much more so than others I have known better and where I have stayed longer. This is particularly true of the road to Emmaus, walking along which with a friend I found myself living unforgettably through the experiences of the two travellers who took the same road shortly after the Crucifixion, as described in the New Testament. So much so that thenceforth I have never doubted that, wherever the walk and whoever the wayfarers, there is always, as on that other occasion on the road to Emmaus, a third presence ready to emerge from the shadows and fall in step along the dusty, stony way.

The actual circumstances of the Holy Land, it is true, were quite different when I was there from in Renan's time. Then, it was part of the Ottoman Empire, and the Galileans whose idyllic way of life Renan had so gushed over were predominantly what we now call Arabs; whereas by the time we came to do our filming, the State of Israel had so consolidated its position that, after many centuries of exile, servitude and dispersal, Jews were again in control of Jerusalem. The role of the Roman legionaries had been taken over by the Israeli army. Now it was the Arabs who were in the position of a subject people; entitled, like the Jews in Jesus's lifetime, to attend their mosques and practise their religion, but otherwise treated like second-class citizens.

Despite these so different circumstances, like Renan I, too, found that just being in the Holy Land somehow consolidated and animated the story of Jesus as told in the Gospels. Whereas, however, in his case the effect had been to bring the story down to earth, making, as it were, a pastoral out of a Mystery play, in my case it worked the other way round: it was the Mystery that came to life. Renan's amiable *devin du village* was lost in the stupendous drama of Golgotha, whose scene – Jerusalem, that tragic city – continued, as far as I was concerned, to convey some special flavour of eternity despite the shouts of hucksters and money-changers, still at their old trade and in approximately the same place as when Jesus chastised them; despite the patter of guides and the tourists endlessly processing along a Via Dolorosa that has become a Via Curiosa. The Holy Land is full of history, written in stones, and with the faces in the streets for alphabet. Yet it was not history I found there, but some other deeper and more exhilarating truth that lay beneath the stones, the faces and all the hubbub and the fraudulence.

I remember the precise moment of illumination very well. It was in the Church of the Nativity in Bethlehem. I was sitting in the crypt waiting for the time when the public were excluded and we could begin to film. Earlier in the day we had been filming in nearby fields where, reputedly, shepherds were tending their flocks when they heard the tidings of great joy, that a Saviour had been born in Bethlehem whom they would find there in a manger wrapped in swaddling clothes. Sure enough, in the fields there was a shepherd with his flock – sheep and goats duly separated, just as required. When he caught sight of us and our equipment he picked up one of his sheep in his arms, precisely as in the coloured pictures I remembered so well from Scripture lessons in my childhood. Then, when he had established his posture, and our cameraman was focusing for a shot, he put down the sheep and came forward to haggle over his fee. It was after settling this unseemly transaction, and getting our footage of the shepherd and his flock, that we went into the Church of the Nativity, having the greatest difficulty in making our way because of the press of beggars and children offering picture post-cards, rosaries and other souvenirs for sale.

Still smarting from their persistent importunity, I had found a seat in the crypt on a stone ledge in the shadow cast by the lighted candles which provided the only illumination. How ridiculous these so-called 'shrines' were!, I was thinking to myself. How squalid the commercialism which exploited them! Who but a credulous fool could possibly suppose that the place marked in the crypt with a silver cross was veritably the precise spot where Jesus had been born? The Holy

Land, as it seemed to me, had been turned into a sort of Jesusland, on the lines of Disneyland.

Everything in the crypt – the garish hangings which covered the stone walls, the tawdry crucifixes and pictures and hanging lamps – was conducive to such a mood. The essential point, after all, about Jesus's birth was its obscurity, which made a perfect contrast with an Aphrodite rising in all her beauty and splendour out of the sea, or an Apollo radiant and masterful even by comparison with his fellow deities. How foolish and inappropriate, then, even from the point of view of fabricating a shrine, to furbish up what purported to be Jesus's birthplace with stage effects, decking out his bare manger to look like a junk-shop crammed with discarded ecclesiastical bric-à-brac! Rather, the shrine should surely aim at accentuating the bareness, the lowliness, of the occasion it celebrated, so that the humblest, poorest visitor might know that the Son of God was born into the world in even humbler, poorer circumstances than his.

As these thoughts passed through my mind I began to notice the demeanour of the visitors coming into the crypt. Some crossed themselves; a few knelt down; most were obviously standard twentieth-century pursuers of happiness for whom the Church of the Nativity was just an item in a sightseeing tour – as it might be the Taj Mahal, or the Chamber of Horrors in Madame Tussaud's Waxworks Show in London, or Lenin's embalmed corpse in his mausoleum in the Red Square in Moscow. None the less, as I observed, each face as it came into view was in some degree transfigured by the experience of being in what purported to be the actual scene of Jesus's birth. This, they all seemed to be saying, was where it happened; here he came into the world! here we shall find him! The boredom, the idle curiosity, the vagrant thinking all disappeared. Once more in that place glory shone around, and angel voices proclaimed: *Unto you is born this day ... a Saviour, which is Christ the Lord!*, thereby transforming it from a tourist attraction into an authentic shrine. 'Everything possible to be believed is an image of truth', Blake wrote. And: 'Truth can never be told so as to be understood and not be believed.' The story of Jesus as recounted in the Gospels is true to the degree that it can be, and is, believed; its truth must be looked for in the hearts of believers rather than in history, or in archaeological dust or anthropological bones. *Where two or three are gathered together in my name*, Jesus promised, *there I am in the midst of them.* The promise has been kept even in the unlikeliest of places – his own ostensible birthplace in the crypt of the Church of the Nativity in Bethlehem.

Looking for Jesus in history is as futile as trying to invent a yardstick that will measure infinity, or a clock that will tick through eternity. God moulds history to His purposes, revealing in it the Fearful Symmetry which is His language in conversing with men; but history is no more than the clay in which He works. Who would look for Michelangelo's *Pietà* in the quarry where the marble to make it was procured? Or for Shakespeare's King Lear in history? If this is true of mortal genius, how much more so when the artist is God Himself, concerned to send us a self-portrait in the lineaments, and using the language, of mortality in order to open up for us new vistas of hope and understanding. This was the Incarnation, described in the opening words of the Fourth Gospel, in a passage surely among the greatest ever to be written at any time or by any hand. From its triumphant opening: *In the beginning was the Word, and the Word was with God, and the Word was God*, to its beautiful and comforting conclusion: *And the Word was made flesh, and dwelt among us . . . full of grace and truth*, it conveys with perfect clarity why the Incarnation had to be, and what it meant for mankind, at the time and for ever after.

*   *   *

So the story of Jesus has to begin with the Incarnation; without it, there would be no story at all. Plenty of great teachers, mystics, martyrs and saints have made their appearance at different times in the world, and lived lives and spoken words full of grace and truth, for which we have every reason to be grateful. Of none of them, however, has the claim been made, and accepted, that they were Incarnate God. In the case of Jesus alone the belief has persisted that when he came into the world God deigned to take on the likeness of a man in order that thenceforth men might be encouraged to aspire after the likeness of God; reaching out from their mortality to His immortality, from their imperfection to His perfection. It is written in the Old Testament that no man may see God and live; at the same time, as Kierkegaard points out, God cannot make Man His equal without transforming him into something more than Man. The only solution was for God to become Man, which He did through the Incarnation in the person of Jesus. Thereby, He set a window in the tiny dark dungeon of the ego in which we all languish, letting in a light, providing a vista, and offering a way of release from the servitude of the flesh and the fury of the will into what St Paul called *the glorious liberty of the children of God*.

This is what the Incarnation, realized in the birth of Jesus, and in the drama of his ministry, death and Resurrection, was to signify. With it, Eternity steps into Time, and Time loses itself in Eternity.

Hence Jesus; in the eyes of God, a man, and in the eyes of men, God. It is sublimely simple; a transcendental soap-opera going on century after century and touching innumerable hearts; from some bleak, lonely soul seeking a hand to hold when all others have been withdrawn, to vast concourses of joyful believers singing their *glorias*, their *kyries*, their *misereres*. There have been endless variations in the script, in the music, in the dialogue, but one thing remains constant – the central figure, Jesus. After the great Jehovah before whose wrath even the gentiles bow down, the Lamb of God; after the immutable Law handed down to Moses from on high, grace and truth embodied in a gospel of love; after the Creation, the Incarnation, when the momentous announcement: *Fiat Lux!* which begins our human story finds its fulfilment in another: *Ecce Homo!* Let there be Light!, and then: Behold the Man! With the Light came the universe, and all its creatures; illimitable space to be explored, and the tiniest atoms to be broken down into yet tinier ones. With the Incarnation came the Man, and the addition of a new spiritual dimension to the cosmic scene. The universe provides a stage; Jesus is the play.

The exigencies of the play require that his birth shall be both miraculous and ordinary. Wise Men attend it, and also shepherds; a new star announces it, and yet it takes place in the lowliest of circumstances – in a manger, with the beasts of the field that are housed there looking on expressionlessly as Jesus emerges from his mother's womb. Gifts of gold, frankincense and myrrh signify a royal birth, the coming of a prince of the House of David; the homely greetings of the shepherds welcome a friend of the poor, the lowly and the oppressed – a man for others. Similarly, Mary, in delivering Incarnate God into the dangerous world, has to be, at once, the most radiant and warm-blooded of mothers whose breasts gush with milk, and a virgin untouched by any sensual hand or carnal experience. The Holy Child has to come, fleshly, out of her flesh, and, at the same time, not through fleshly processes. As she proclaims in her *Magnificat*, God has regarded her lowliness, and made her blessed in the eyes of future generations, by bestowing upon her the inestimable privilege that in her womb the Incarnation happens.

Until comparatively recent times Christians found little difficulty in combining these two themes of perfect motherhood and perfect virginity. The Madonnas of the Middle Ages, endlessly painted, sculpted, celebrated in verse and prose and Plainsong, are glowingly alive without being involved in our human concupiscence. One comes across them in obscure churches as in great cathedrals and abbeys – faces of transcendental beauty that are also enchantingly

And the angel came in unto her, and said, Hail, thou that art highly favoured, the Lord is with thee : blessed art thou among women.

EMBROIDERY, THIRTEENTH CENTURY

homely, and even droll, in wood and stone and marble; still with candle flames flickering in front of them and flowers heaped before them, and a few figures kneeling, touched with wonder at a Mother of God, who was, at once, so sublimely motherly, and so humanly divine. Such faces, blending physical and spiritual beauty into a sort of celestial coquetry, are likewise to be seen among nuns – or were until they put aside their habits and rules to follow Demas and the fashions of this present world. In humanistic times like ours, a contemporary virgin – assuming there are any such – would regard a message from the Angel Gabriel that she might expect to give birth to a son to be called the Son of the Highest as ill-tidings of great sorrow and a slur on the local family-planning centre. It is, in point of fact, extremely improbable, under existing conditions, that Jesus would have been permitted to be born at all. Mary's pregnancy, in poor circumstances, and with the father unknown, would have been an obvious case for an abortion; and her talk of having conceived as a result of the intervention of the Holy Ghost would have pointed to the need for psychiatric treatment, and made the case for terminating her pregnancy even stronger. Thus our generation, needing a Saviour more, perhaps, than any that has ever existed, would be too humane to allow one to be born; too enlightened to permit the Light of the World to shine in a darkness that grows ever more oppressive.

To a twentieth-century mind the notion of a virgin birth is intrinsically and preposterously inconceivable. If a woman claims – such claims are made from time to time – to have become pregnant without sexual intercourse, no one believes her. Yet for centuries millions upon millions of people never doubted that Mary had begotten Jesus without the participation of a husband or lover. Nor was such a belief limited to the simple and unlettered; the most profound and most erudite minds, the greatest artists and craftsmen, found no difficulty in accepting the Virgin Birth as an incontestable fact – for instance, Pascal, who in the versatility of his gifts and the originality of his insights was regarded as the Aristotle of his time. From a contemporary point of view, this is the more surprising in that little effort would seem to have been made to achieve consistency or credibility in the account in the Gospels of Jesus's birth. Thus, the genealogical table purporting to establish Jesus's descent from King David in accordance with Messianic prophecy is traced through Joseph, with whom, if the Virgin Birth really happened, he had no blood relationship.

Are we, then, to suppose that our forebears who believed implicitly in the Virgin Birth were gullible fools, whereas we, who would no more believe in such notions than we would that the world is flat, have put aside childish things and become mature? Is our scepticism one more manifestation of our having – in Bonhoeffer's unhappy phrase – come of age? It would be difficult to support such a proposition in the light of the almost inconceivable credulity of today's brain-washed public, who so readily believe absurdities in advertisements and in statistical and sociological prognostications before which an African witch-doctor would recoil in derision. With Pascal it was the other way round; while accepting, with the same certainty as he did the coming of the seasons, the New Testament account of Jesus's birth, he had already seen through and scornfully rejected the pretensions of science. Now, three centuries later, his intuition has been amply fulfilled. The dogmatism of science has become a new orthodoxy, disseminated by the Media and a State educational system with a thoroughness and subtlety far exceeding anything of the kind achieved by the Inquisition; to the point that to believe today in a miraculous happening like the Virgin Birth is to appear a kind of imbecile, whereas to disbelieve in an unproven and unprovable scientific proposition like the Theory of Evolution, and still more to question some quasi-scientific shibboleth like the Population Explosion, is to stand condemned as an obscurantist, an enemy of progress and enlightenment.

Does this mean that we must consider Pascal as having been, in his scientific capacity, an admitted genius, but, in his capacity of apologist for the Christian religion, a credulous fool? Is his work on the vacuum, his invention of the computer, of dazzling originality, but his *Pensées* no more than the vain imaginings of a naturally sceptical mind seeking for transcendental certainties at any cost? On the contrary, it is through the *Pensées* that his fame has been kept alive; it is to the *Pensées* that innumerable seekers after truth, up to and including our own time, have turned for enlightenment and inspiration, and never in vain. The key to this seeming disparity between Pascal the scientist, scrupulously observing facts and weighing their relevance, and Pascal the Christian, bowing his head, bending his knees, humbling his proud mind, before the Virgin Mother of Jesus, lies in the one word 'faith': what the writer of the Epistle to the Hebrews called *the substance of things hoped for, the evidence of things not seen*. Faith that bridges the chasm between what our minds can know and what our souls aspire after; faith which so dwarfs whatever we may consider ourselves to have achieved, or been, that it makes all men – the humblest, the simplest, the most, in worldly terms, foolish – our equals, our brothers; faith which so irradiates our inner being and

And the Word was made flesh, and dwelt among us.

PAINTING BY GEERTGEN

20

Behold, there came wise men from the east to Jerusalem, Saying, Where is he that is born King of the Jews? . . . And there were in the same country shepherds abiding in the field, keeping watch over their flock by night.

DETAIL OF ALTARPIECE, PAINTED BY MASTER FRANCKE

outward circumstances that the ostensible exactitudes of time and measure, of proof and disproof, lose their precision, existing only in relation to eternal absolutes which everything in the universe proclaims, and in which all life has its being – the stones and the creatures, the pig's grunt and the nightingale's song, the trees and the mountains, the wind and the clouds, height and depth, darkness and light, everything that ever has been, or ever will be, attempted, or done, till the end of time – all swelling the chorus of faith.

It was precisely to revivify and replenish the world's stock of faith that the Bethlehem birth took place. Seen with the eye of faith, the shepherds rejoice, the Wise Men prostrate themselves and offer their gifts, the very stars are rearranged – though I have always considered myself that it was probably the Morning Star in its familiar place that the Wise Men followed, shining so wondrously on that momentous occasion that it was taken to be a new intruder into the heavens. Seen with the eye of faith, everything falls perfectly into place, faith being the key which enables us to decipher God's otherwise inscrutable communications. The centrepiece is, of course, Mary, a Virgin Mother, with God sucking voraciously at her breast; bearing in her arms the new light that has come into the world to lighten, not just the Jews, but the Gentiles, all mankind, as well. So it has been celebrated year by year through the centuries of Christendom, in carols, in crèches, in plays and processions, in a combination of public worship and private acts of giving, until now, when faith seems to be expiring, and the light has grown correspondingly dim, it has become a mighty exercise in salesmanship, a gala occasion in the great contemporary cult of consumption, an act of worship directed towards our latest deity – the Gross National Product.

Apart from the one dubious reference in Josephus, in his own lifetime Jesus made no impact on history. This is something that I cannot but regard as a special dispensation on God's part, and, I like to think, yet another example of the ironical humour which informs so many of His purposes. To me, it seems highly appropriate that the most important figure in all history should thus escape the notice of memoirists, diarists, commentators, all the tribe of chroniclers who even then existed, and, four centuries later, were so scarified by St Augustine in the days when he held what he called his 'Chair of Lies' in Milan. Historically, Jesus is, strictly speaking, a non-person. Anthropologically, too, he is without interest; we know, in this respect, more about Neanderthal Man than about the Son of Man. Likewise, sociologically Jesus is a non-starter. What did he earn? How did he vote? What examinations did he pass, and what countries

did he visit? The Gospels do not tell us, and we have no other means of knowing, though this has not prevented invention from getting to work; even, of late, in the Kinsey field. A suffragan Anglican bishop has raised the question of whether Jesus may not have been a homosexual; a sometime theological instructor in Manchester has devised a theory, with all the ostensible appurtenances of scholarship, whereby the Gospels are no more than a phallic code; and in Scandinavia – inevitably there! – film-makers have turned their attention to Jesus's sex-life. Truly the myths of fact are the most absurd and misleading of all – this being, perhaps, designed by God to humble our pride when we discover that the myths of faith turn out to be, by comparison, our only truth. Even the most conscientious historians can study the past, as geologists do, only through its fossils; truth belongs essentially

Behold, from henceforth all generations shall call me blessed.

PAINTING BY BELLINI

24

to a spiritual order where the categories of time and space, without which history cannot exist, are inapplicable. History is too fragile and indeterminate a structure to contain Jesus; like – using the imagery of one of his own parables – the old wineskins into which new wine cannot be put, or like the worn cloth which cannot be patched with new. How shabby, how patched and repatched, how threadbare and faded this fabric of history is, compared with the ever-renewed, gleaming and glistening garment of truth!

Through the eye of faith, then, Jesus is seen as, at once, God and Man, as Mary is seen as, at once, Virgin and Mother. His perfect humanity and perfect godhead combine, as do her perfect virginity and perfect motherhood, to produce, in the one case, the Son of God, in the other, the Mother of God. Suddenly, almost with a click, like a film coming into sync, everything has meaning, everything is real; and the meaning, the reality, shine out in every shape and sound and movement, in each and every manifestation of life, so that I want to cry out with the blind man to whom Jesus restored his sight: *One thing I know, that, whereas I was blind, now I see.* How, I ask myself, could I have missed it before? How not have understood that the grey-silver light across the water, the cry of the sea-gulls and the sweep of their wings, everything on which my eyes rest and my ears hear, is telling me about God.

> This life's dim Windows of the Soul
> Distorts the Heavens from Pole to Pole
> And leads you to believe a Lie
> When you see with, not thro', the Eye.

Thus Blake distinguishes between the fantasy that is seen with the eye and the truth that is seen through it. They are two clearly demarcated kingdoms; and passing from one to the other, from the kingdom of fantasy to the kingdom of reality, gives inexpressible delight. As when the sun comes out, and a dark landscape is suddenly glorified, all that was obscure becoming clear, all that was incomprehensible, comprehensible. Fantasy's joys and desires dissolve away, and in their place is one joy, one desire; one Oneness – God. In this kingdom of reality, Simone Weil tells us, nothing is so continually fresh and surprising, so full of sweet and perpetual ecstasy, as goodness; no desert so dreary, monotonous and boring as evil. There we may understand what St Augustine meant when he insisted that 'though the higher things are better than the lower, the sum of all creation is better than the higher things alone', and how, in the light of this realization, all human progress, human morality, human law, based, as they are, on the opposite proposition – of the

intrinsic superiority of the higher over the lower – is seen as written on water, scribbled on dust; like Jesus's scribble while he was waiting for the accusers of the woman taken in adultery to disperse. Alas, then the sun goes in again, and we are back in the kingdom of fantasy, where it is goodness that is flat and boring, and evil that is varied and attractive, profound, intriguing and full of charm. Where the higher is ardently sought on its own account, to be extracted like uranium, pure and unalloyed, from its earthy bed, which is the whole of creation. With how unutterable a longing does one yearn to leave the sunless land of fantasy and live for ever in the sunshine of reality!

Jesus himself makes the same distinction as Blake between what is seen with and through the eye when he directs his teaching specifically to those who have eyes to see and ears to hear. It is not enough, that is to say, just to look and listen; behind the looking and listening there has to be the perspective of faith. Only seeing through the eye, and across this perspective, does the true significance of Jesus and his teaching become clear. Those critics who seek to discover it by minutely and diligently investigating the details of his life, as Tolstoy points out, in reality discover nothing. Even if they were completely successful in their efforts, instead of for the most part trafficking in presumptions and fantasy, and so were able to tell us exactly the sort of person Jesus was, produce a convincing profile of him, they would still be as far as ever from unravelling the secret of his power over the hearts and minds of men, both while he was in the world, and subsequently. This secret is hidden, not in the circumstances of his life, in the people with whom he consorted and the history, superstitions, fashions and ideologies of the time, but in his teaching, at once so pure, so lofty and so simple. It was those luminous words of his, sealed with his death on the Cross, that led to his being recognized as God. After all, who but God would have dared to ask of men what he asked of them? Demanding everything and enduring everything, he set in train a great creative wave of love and sacrifice such as the world had never before seen or dreamed of.

It is commentators like Blake and Tolstoy, Simone Weil and Dostoevsky, who pre-eminently bring Jesus to life, because they approach him through the imagination as artists rather than through the intellect as theologians. In him they observe the very process of art at work in the Word becoming flesh and dwelling among us full of grace and truth, and are no more concerned to discover him as an historical personage than they would be to go through the records of La Mancha for traces of Don Quixote's lineage, or through Burke's *Landed Gentry* for traces of Falstaff's. The process itself

27

*Mary kept all these
things, and pondered
them in her heart.*

PAINTING BY VAN
ROYMERSWAELE

– making the Word flesh and vesting it with grace and truth –
suffices. This is what every artist is endlessly seeking to do. Thus
Jesus's story is a drama, not documentation, and the Word whose
flesh he became is every true word ever written or spoken; every
true note ever sounded, every true stone laid on another, every
true shape moulded or true colour mixed. The whole creative
achievement of Man is comprehended in it. Look for it in the light
shining in El Greco's faces; listen for it in the notes of Plainsong;
marvel at it in the spire of Salisbury Cathedral rising so exquisitely
into the sky; read it in Blake's *Songs of Innocence* and *Songs of
Experience*. Hold it in your hand in a grain of sand; in your mind in
the universe, with all its planetary systems within systems, and
ultimate vistas of everlasting space; in your soul in the contemplation
of the creator of it all, the spirit which animates it all, the beginning
and the end of what has no beginning and no end – God. Then,
pinpoint it all, bring it all to a focus, concentrate it all in a Man, and
that Man – Jesus.

However, wherever and in whatever circumstances Jesus was born,
there was, we may be sure, a real baby, wrinkled and wizened and full
of wind, as babies are, and a doting mother to offer her breast, and
look down with pride and joy at the tiny head of the little creature
ardently sucking at it. Though in our time motherhood has been
greatly devalued, and the sick phrase 'unwanted child' been given
currency, it still remains true, as any nurse or gynaecologist will
confirm, that it is extremely rare for any child at the moment of
birth to be other than wanted in its mother's eyes. Once when I was
in Calcutta with Mother Teresa she picked up one of the so-called
'unwanted' babies which had come into the care of her Missionaries of
Charity. It had been salvaged from a dustbin, and was so minute that
one wondered it could exist at all. When I remarked on this, a look
of exultation came into Mother Teresa's face. 'See,' she said, 'there's
life in it!' So there was; and suddenly it was as though I were present
at the Bethlehem birth, and the baby Mother Teresa was holding
another Lamb of God sent into the world to lighten our darkness.
How could we know? How dared we prognosticate upon what made
life worth while for this or that child? How many Lambs of God may
not have been carried away in buckets of hospital waste?

Mary's joy and pride in the baby Jesus sucking at her breast will
naturally have been magnified by the knowledge that had been
conveyed to her of the great destiny awaiting this particular child;
but her rejoicing would have been very great anyway. Every mother's
son, particularly the first-born, is a Son of God; a miraculous being

29

whose arrival in the world is a unique occasion, with great things lying ahead. If God chose to become incarnate as Jesus, then his birth, whatever marvels may have accompanied it, must have had the same characteristics as any other; just as, on the Cross, the suffering of the man into whom the Bethlehem child grew must have been of the same nature as that of the two delinquents crucified beside him. Otherwise, Jesus's humanity would have been a fraud; in which case, his divinity would have been fraudulent, too. The perfection of Jesus's divinity was expressed in the perfection of his humanity, and vice versa. He was God because he was so sublimely a man, and Man because, in all his sayings and doings, in the grace of his person and words, in the love and compassion that shone out of him, he walked so closely with God. As Man alone, Jesus could not have saved us; as God alone, he would not; Incarnate, he could and did.

Joseph and Mary had come to Bethlehem despite the lack of accommodation because, we are told, their presence was required there for a census that was being taken. Here, the finger of history momentarily intrudes. There was, it seems, some sort of census being taken round about this time by Caesar Augustus, then at the height of his fame. He had already been proclaimed a god, with appropriate rites for worshipping him; and his régime was considered to be so enlightened, stable and prosperous that it would go on for ever – a final solution to the problem of government and a guarantee of the continuing happiness and prosperity of all who were fortunate enough to be Roman citizens. Expiring civilizations are prone to such fantasies; for instance, ours, notable in the last half century, equally, for inane hope and inane despair. Of all the millions of souls numbered in Caesar Augustus's census, the one born in Bethlehem just in time to be included in it must have been, in wordly terms, about the most insignificant, and the least likely to figure, in the estimation of posterity, as having any comparable importance with that of the great Emperor. It was a confrontation of sorts between the man who passed for being the ruler of the world and the latest and lowliest of his subjects. Yet, of course, as it turned out, their roles were to be reversed; for centuries to come Jesus would reign over men's minds and hearts, when Augustus's kingdom existed only in history books and ruins. Was it, I have often wondered, Augustus's head – it might have been, though by then Tiberius was reigning – on the coin that was produced apropos one of Jesus's most famous observations, about rendering unto Caesar the things that are Caesar's and unto God the things that are God's? If so, it would have

Behold, the angel of the Lord appeareth to Joseph in a dream, saying, Arise, and take the young child and his mother, and flee into Egypt.
PAINTING BY SIDNEY NOLAN

30

been appropriate enough; Augustus being a Caesar who claimed to be a god, and Jesus being God in the likeness of a man.

After Jesus's birth, we are told, Joseph and Mary took him into Egypt. The occasion for the journey had prophetic support in the beautiful lines of Jeremiah: *A voice was heard in Ramah, lamentation, and bitter weeping; Rachel weeping for her children refused to be comforted, . . . because they were not.* This is taken as referring to a decree by King Herod that all children of two years old and under in the neighbourhood of Bethlehem should be put to death. Thereby he hoped to ensure the elimination of the child of the House of David destined to be King of the Jews, about whose prophesied birth the Wise Men had told him, and in whom he saw a possible rival. It was Herod who, in the first place, sent the Wise Men to spy out the land in Bethlehem, with strict instructions to report back to him on what they found there. Having found Jesus, being Wise Men, they decided that it would be more prudent to return to the Orient whence they came by another route that did not take in a return visit to Herod. They are portrayed as *Magi*, or magicians, skilled in reading the stars and in soothsaying, by the early illustrators of the New Testament in their exquisite Books of Hours and illuminated manuscripts and Missals. I prefer to think of them in contemporary guise as pundits or talking heads; a think-tank, or Brains Trust, an *Any Questions* team. Do the panel think . . . ? In any case, having circumvented Herod's domain, the Wise Men disappear from view, leaving him to order the Massacre of the Innocents, another episode popular with early Christian illustrators. Sceptics who wonder if anything of the kind ever happened may reflect that Herod's efforts are quite put in the shade today, when for the highest humanitarian motives babies are slaughtered on an infinitely larger scale than ever he managed, even before they have left the womb – something Herod did not think of.

The episode of the Flight to Egypt, like numerous others in the Gospels, doubtless owes much to the fact that it may be taken as fulfilling a Jewish prophecy – *Out of Egypt did I call my son.* This notion of taking deliberate steps, actually devising events, in order that a prophecy might seem to have been fulfilled, was one of my earliest Biblical enigmas. If, I remember reflecting as a child, and perhaps asking some unfortunate teacher, this or that had to be done to fulfil a prophecy, how was it a prophecy at all? Surely, prophesying meant foreseeing something that was going to happen, not so arranging things that it happened. Subsequent experience of life, and brooding thereon, made me understand that two parallel processes are at work – prophesying, and surrendering to the logic of events whereby the prophecy comes to pass. Built into our mortal circumstances there is what Blake called a Fearful Symmetry –

> Tyger, Tyger, burning bright
> In the forests of the night,
> What immortal hand or eye
> Dare frame thy fearful symmetry?

– which, once understood, makes it possible to envisage the consequences of things. Thus, a sunflower seed has a built-in propensity to become a sunflower, spreading its yellow petals, and, as Blake so beautifully puts it, becoming weary of time as it counts the steps of the sun. Equally, to realize this propensity, unfold this Fearful Symmetry, the sunflower has to be planted and watered and nurtured. The Old Testament prophets, attuned to the Fearful Symmetry of God's purposes, are able to announce what lies ahead – the mercies and the glories and the wrath to come. As with the sunflower, however, in order that their prophecies may be fulfilled, the ground has to be prepared and watered; the young shoots, or embryonic happenings, have to be nurtured and helped to grow and develop into their full historical fulfilment. Likewise with more recent prophets like Dostoevsky, who saw with extraordinary clarity as being implicit in the Russian scene, in the ramshackle texture and romantic credulity of the European liberal mind, the revolutionary upheaval that loomed ahead. In conveying this in his writings – notably in his novel *The Devils* – he facilitated its inevitable coming-to-pass. Again, Kierkegaard envisaged with uncanny precision just what the consequences of universal suffrage democracy, mass Media and the pursuit of happiness through material wellbeing and sensual indulgence were bound to be, and how the Christian Churches in these circumstances would be diverted into proclaiming an earthly kingdom, and so destroy themselves. Like the prophets of old, in so forcefully and correctly forecasting the future, he helped to bring it about; 'In order that the prophecy might be fulfilled' would have been a suitable epitaph to inscribe on his tomb, especially appropriate in present-day Copenhagen, his native city.

Similarly, it has become abundantly clear in the second half of the twentieth century that Western Man has decided to abolish himself. Having wearied of the struggle to be himself, he has created his own boredom out of his own affluence, his own impotence out of his own erotomania, his own vulnerability out of his own strength; himself blowing the trumpet that brings the walls of his own city tumbling down, and, in a process of auto-genocide, convincing himself that he is too numerous, and labouring accordingly with pill and scalpel and syringe to make himself fewer in order to be an easier prey for his enemies; until at last, having educated himself into imbecility, and polluted and drugged himself into stupefaction, he keels over, a weary, battered old brontosaurus, and becomes extinct. Many, like Spengler, have envisaged the future in such terms, and now what they prophesied is upon us.

The writers of the Gospels see the drama of Jesus's life and death as likewise a fulfilment of prophecy. Indeed, they portray him as shaping the happenings of his life, and even the words he spoke in the course of his ministry, to the exigencies of the Messianic expectations of the Hebrew prophets. Thereby they provided a validation of Jesus's mission in the world that was in keeping with Jewish tradition, and so particularly acceptable to Synagogue-trained minds. St Paul, for instance, on his missionary journeys, was much given to stressing Jesus's impeccable credentials as the expected Messiah. In their exposition of the fulfilment of prophecy the Gospels faithfully reflect the mysterious blend of determinism and freedom which governs our lives. What happens, they tell us, has to happen, but still need not; we must bend our knees and bow our heads and say *Thy will be done*, while none the less knowing, as Jesus did in his dark hour in the Garden of Gethsemane, that it is open to us to follow our own wills. The demons of the ego are allowed to enter into us, as they were allowed to enter into the Gadarene swine, and can send us similarly leaping to destruction.

The imagination can relate these two seeming opposites – determinism and freedom – into a wholeness which partakes of both and is greater than either. Hence art. Watching a performance, say, of *Macbeth*, we know perfectly well that Macbeth will murder Duncan, and all the tragic consequences that will ensue, and yet hang breathlessly on Macbeth's words as he summons up his resolution to fulfil the witches' prediction. The intellect, on the other hand, drops an iron curtain between determinism and freedom, resulting, at one end of the scale, in the phantasmagoria of total determinism, whereby all our destiny, individual and collective, is comprehended in genes which nothing can alter or affect except pure chance – Caliban's conclusion, incidentally – and, at the other end of the scale, in the corresponding phantasmagoria of total freedom in terms of unrestrained violence, animality and chaos. Prophecy belongs to the domain of the imagination, not of the intellect; its truth lies in the inescapable necessity to fulfil it; its strength, in our sense that we are free to fulfil it or not as we think fit. This is why, especially at moments of great crisis in our individual lives or in history, we often seem to be following a preordained course, and yet choosing, whether grudgingly, heroically, or in desperation, to follow it. From his Bethlehem birth to his death in Jerusalem, Jesus took the road the prophets had marked out, knowing that it would end on Golgotha. If at times he groaned over its ardours, and right at the end asked whether after all he might be let off the final sacrifice, and left a little longer in a world he must have loved or he could not have described and explained it so exquisitely, he always returned to his ultimate prayer: *Not what I will, but what Thou wilt*. This was the theme of his life, the essence of the drama he lived out in order to guide all who came after him in the ways of truth; to give us hope in our despair, and light in our darkness, enabling us to look out from Time, our prison, on to the mercy of Eternity, our liberty.

In 4 BC King Herod, called 'the Great', died, and accordingly, we are told, an angel informed Joseph that it would now be safe for him to return to his homeland with Mary and Jesus. This he did, just to be on the safe side settling in Nazareth in Galilee to keep out of the jurisdiction of Archelaus, Herod's son who had succeeded him as puppet ruler over Judaea. The Emperor Augustus refused to confirm Archelaus's use of the title of 'king' like his father, and in AD 6 deposed him for malpractices and general incompetence, putting his territory under Roman procurators, or governors, of whom Pontius Pilate was the fifth or sixth. His brother, Antipas, was made ruler over Galilee and Peraea. He it was who entered into an illicit relationship with his niece, Herodias, later marrying her while her husband, his brother Philip, was still alive; thereby laying himself open to a furious denunciation by John the Baptist. To punish John, Herod Antipas imprisoned him, according to Josephus, in the Castle of Machaerus, situated by the north-east shore of the Dead Sea, subsequently making a present of his head on a charger to Herodias's daughter, Salome, who had pleased him with an erotic dance. It was Herod Antipas to whom Jesus once referred as *that fox*.

These Herods, unlike Jesus, make their appearance in history. We have their dates, and details of their buffooneries, which interested chroniclers like Josephus, as they would today the Media. They trafficked in the stuff of news – murder, money, fornication, crime, violence and exhibitionism. Nowadays, the cameras would be constantly hovering round them, the gossip-writers and their stringers keeping an eye on them to see what they were up to and who were their latest wives. Herod the Great had ten, and doubtless every one of them yielding a story. 'Bring me the cuttings!', I hear myself saying, and then seem to be thumbing over the bulky envelopeful, noting particularly the great Salome story, so lavishly covered even though a Sunday newspaper had bought exclusive rights from, presumably, Herodias for a very large sum. In contemporary terms, the Herods may be equated with Indian princes in the days of the Raj; rajahs and maharajahs with soft, self-indulgent faces and jewels in their turbans, highnesses who rated gun-salutes and orders and

decorations, and were, like Herod Antipas, highly appreciative of erotic dancing. Ceremonial rather than actual sovereigns, the scavenger dogs of power. And Pontius Pilate – how like a colonial governor! I almost see him in a grey frock-coat and topper; likewise, Caiaphas in lawn sleeves in the House of Lords. These are the pieces in history's running game of chess; the knights and bishops and castles and pawns whose moves are invariable even though the gambits change.

All who have been concerned in the day-by-day reporting of the game's progress – I mean the collection, presentation and dissemination of what is called news – know better than anyone how slight, fragile and fraudulent are the available sources. The bucket dropped into the well of truth is leaky indeed, and such water as it brings up, brackish and polluted. Hurried words shouted down a telephone, tapped out on a teleprinter; then arranged by some other hand to be set up in type or diffused on the waves of sound or vision; as bemusedly received as they have been bemusedly fabricated. *Where shall wisdom be found, and where is the place of understanding?* Not, certainly, in what passes for being the documentation of this or any other age, whether recorded by a Josephus, elegantly recounted by a Gibbon, laboriously assembled by a Namier, dispersed in clouds of rhetoric by a Churchill, or reflected in the fabulous distorting mirror twentieth-century technology has devised to take in every detail and aspect of our contemporary scene – the television screen. This last, least of all; nothing is less actual than its *actualités*. Only mystics, clowns and artists, in my experience, speak the truth, which, as Blake was always insisting, is perceptible to the imagination rather than the mind. Thus an animist grovelling naked in the African bush before a painted stone may well be nearer to the heart of things than any Einstein or Bertrand Russell, and a painted clown riding a bicycle round and round a circus ring more attuned to the reality of life than a Talleyrand or a Bismarck can hope to be. Jesus was making the same point when he insisted that God has revealed to the foolish what is hidden from the wise.

It is a relief to turn from the historical Herods to the mythical Holy Family, travelling from Egypt to the Promised Land, as the Children of Israel once did, with Moses to lead them, and God in the shape of a pillar of fire to show them the way. Traditional Christian artists display a similar preference for the Holy Family over the Herods, and have left many representations of the trio, showing Mary and the baby on a donkey and Joseph striding along beside it. Special loving care is given to the donkey, in whose patient countenance one may detect a quiet satisfaction, even a touch of pride, at having had a role on so notable an occasion. Indeed, it is one of Christianity's minor, but still most estimable, services to have raised these dear beasts from a somewhat lowly position in the animal hierarchy to a share in the glory of the first Palm Sunday. G. K. Chesterton has celebrated their rise in the world in a well-known poem, and to this day in the Middle East, as they toil, heavy-laden, along the same dusty roads as in Jesus's time, they wear an expression which seems to be saying: What these old eyes have seen and these long ears have heard! Riding on them sometimes on Middle Eastern journeys, conscious of their sturdy backs and steady tread, I have felt myself to be somehow participating in their self-esteem.

Of the years between the Holy Family's settling in Nazareth and the beginning of Jesus's ministry, the Gospels tell us nothing, apart from one episode in St Luke's Gospel concerning a visit to Jerusalem when Jesus was still a child to attend the Feast of the Passover. According to this account, on the return journey Jesus was found to be missing, and Joseph and Mary had to go back to Jerusalem and look for him. They found him in the Temple sitting in the midst of the learned doctors, listening to them and asking them questions, and generally amazing them by his knowledge of the Scriptures and quick-wittedness.

Why do the Gospels thus neglect Jesus's youth and young manhood? Was it because their writers knew nothing about this formative period of his life? Or because, as far as their purpose was concerned, they did not think it mattered much? Probably the latter. After all, they were not writing biographies, but recording the sayings and doings of Jesus, as handed down verbally from eyewitness or traditional accounts, for the purpose of carrying out his basic command to his followers – to spread his words and teaching far and wide to prepare people for the coming of his kingdom, for the new era he had ushered in. The purpose of the writers of the Gospels, in other words, was evangelism, not biography or documentation. Thus, all four of them give, biographically speaking, a quite disproportionate amount of space to the last few days of Jesus's life, when he was betrayed, interrogated, tried and executed; but from the point of view of their evangelistic purpose, this was justified. The Christian congregations springing up everywhere for whom they essentially wrote needed to know as much as possible about the Passion and the Resurrection, the heart of their new faith. So the Gospels harvest every word they can get hold of about those last days, and more or less ignore the first thirty years of Jesus's life. The traditional Christian artists were

And all that heard him were astonished at his understanding and answers.

PART OF ALTAR PANEL, PAINTED BY MASTER BERTRAM

well content to follow them in this; it was only in the nineteenth century that invention came into play, and idealized versions of the Nazareth carpenter's shop began to figure. When faith goes, sentimentality rather than scepticism fills the resultant vacuum; and there is not so much a suspension of belief as a readiness to believe anything. Jesus deposed from the Godhead becomes Jesus Superstar, an infinitely less credible figure.

In this sense, the absence from the Gospels of material relating to Jesus's early years may be taken as an intimation of their authenticity. If they had been faked with a view to supporting the doctrines and superstitions of the early Church, why not include fabricated anecdotes designed to show how Jesus's sense of having a special destiny in the world, and a special son-father relationship with God, was manifest even in childhood? Such anecdotes, as any professional gossip-writer or hagiographer knows, are easy to invent and always go down well; in popular biographical writing about the heroes of our time they abound, as, indeed, in the early Christian apocryphal gospels. They are easily invented, rarely denied, and give pleasure to all. One of the things that has struck me about the New Testament Gospels altogether is how very easy it would have been to sub-edit them so as to eliminate the contradictions, inconsistencies and occasional apparent absurdities which have so delighted agnostics and whose exegesis has so exercised commentators. I really believe that, given a free hand and some expert help, I could have done the job myself in quite a short time, producing a consistent story with nothing in it for critics to cavil at or sceptics to ridicule. That this was not done when the first definitive texts were prepared – it would have been so easy then – suggests strongly to me that the writers of the Gospels believed they were recording Jesus's very words and deeds as handed down by eyewitnesses. They felt themselves to be in some special way Jesus's amanuensis rather than his chronicler, and therefore precluded from trying to work out and rearrange their material in order to make it more cogent and palatable; still more from altering it for the doctrinal convenience of the early Church.

One thing is clear to an old journalist who has done his fair share of putting garbled or 'awkward' copy into shape – if the Gospels are a fake, then the hands that did the faking were quite exceptionally inexpert and careless. All I can say myself, who am no scholar, and as unconcerned about the textual and other conundrums to which theologians and Biblical scholars so earnestly and diligently address themselves as about Shakespeare's mistaken assumption that Bohemia had a coastline, is that, on closer acquaintance with the

And the child grew, and waxed strong in spirit, filled with wisdom: and the grace of God was upon him.

PAINTING BY MILLAIS

Gospels, my sense of their beauty and sublimity has grown ever greater. Likewise, my conviction that they are, in the truest and most literal sense of the word, inspired, in their portrayal of the central character, Jesus – the words he spoke, the life he lived, the death he died and the deathlessness he exemplified. In this connection, I find it reassuring that J. B. Phillips should, after his long, arduous labours at preparing his own version of the New Testament, have reached a similar conclusion, as he movingly testifies in his book *The Ring of Truth*.

Another deduction to be made from the absence of traditional anecdotes relating to Jesus's early years is that the qualities which made him in later life so noticeable, and in the end notorious, had not by then shown themselves. What was exceptional in him would seem to have become apparent only when he embarked on his ministry. Had it been otherwise, we may be sure there would have been a whole body of legendary tales of the kind Luke gives about his encounter as a child with the learned doctors in the Temple. The one person who knew of the special destiny that awaited him, and noted intimations of it, was Mary, his mother, but she, we are told, kept this knowledge in her heart. Others would not have noticed, so that in Nazareth Jesus passed for being the perfectly ordinary son of Joseph. Hence the sense of outrage caused by his address in the Nazareth synagogue, when he spoke of his Messianic role in the world – *Is not this the carpenter's son? Is not his mother called Mary, and his brethren, James, and Joses, and Simon, and Judas? And his sisters, are they not all with us? Whence, then, hath this man all these things?*

Numerous attempts have been made to compensate for this lack of any information about Jesus's childhood and early manhood in the Gospels by trying to reconstruct the kind of life a carpenter's son might be expected to have had in Nazareth in the last years of Caesar Augustus's and the first years of Tiberius's reigns. Such reconstructions, despite their ostensible objectivity, are liable to be highly subjective; it is not only where our treasure is, but where our heroes are, that our heart is also. Thus, the Victorian Jesus, working in Joseph's workshop, is shown as the prototype of the Good Apprentice, diligent and skilful at his trade of carpenter, virtuous in his ways, and belonging to the family of a prosperous artisan who might be considered more a jobbing builder than a mere carpenter. Some countenance for this is said to be provided in the parables about building houses on firm foundations, and other vaguely constructional or architectural references attributed to Jesus.

The fact is, of course, that we have no reliable means of knowing what Jesus's circumstances were until the Gospels pick up the story of his ministry. The various data by which we categorize people are just not applicable in his case. Jesus, anyway, stands apart from all categories, earthly and heavenly alike. Of his intellectual attainments, we know only that he was well versed in the Scriptures, and a brilliant controversialist, skilled at dealing with trick questions and hecklers. The only writing he is reported in the Gospels as doing was with his finger in the dust – not a particularly strong intimation of literacy. From the comment on his teaching in the Temple – *How knoweth this man letters, having never learned?* – it would seem that he was generally regarded as being technically uneducated apart from the regulation studying of the Scriptures under rabbinical direction. This at least is what I like to think, here, I dare say, fashioning a Jesus to my own specifications. His mind, as it seems to me, was too luminous and original, the artistry of his parables, exhortations and addresses too vivid and alive, there was too much sheer genius in him, for him ever to have been subjected to the bridle, bit and blinkers of education. The light he shone before men is rarely seen in the groves of academe; and his insistence on the importance of humility above all other virtues, on seeing with the eye of innocence rather than of knowledge, is not a theme that would go down well among schoolmen at any time. Nor is there in the Gospels any indication that he took the slightest interest in, or had any knowledge of, Roman civilization, of which there were intimations on every hand. He scrupulously refrained from getting mixed up in Jewish nationalism, which was very strong preparatory to the abortive revolt of AD 66–70, particularly in Galilee, and showed no disposition to resent his position as a member of a subject people.

As for the company Jesus kept – it consisted of all sorts and conditions of people, from the rich and important (Nicodemus, Zacchaeus, the Centurion whose favourite servant Jesus healed) to the poor and the outcast. No deductions can be made, therefore, of the sort of company he preferred – if, indeed, he had a preference. He shunned no one, had time to spare for everyone, because his mission was to all mankind. Similarly, there is no indication in the Gospels of any tastes or fancies he might have had; his dedication to his task of spreading the good news that the coming of the Kingdom of God was no longer a remote expectation, but a present reality, was total – the more so because he knew that the time at his disposal was short and would soon run out. We have no notion even of what Jesus looked like; there is not even an apocryphal description of him, as there is of St Paul. The Gospels convey no impression of how he spoke, the timbre of his voice, whether he used gestures and was given to declamation, though in their reports of what he said the style of his utterances is unmistakable. This was sharp, incisive, pungent, often ironic and never rhetorical. He was clearly very observant, both of nature and of men; very aware of how society worked, of the forces of cupidity and aggressiveness which shaped human behaviour. Hence his great gift for vivid imagery, and for telling a story; his parables are little masterpieces of narration, and, like the best of Tolstoy's short stories ('What Men Live By', for instance), easily comprehensible at all levels of understanding. As a communicator pure and simple, I should say that Jesus was supremely effective – this quite apart from his special role and mission in the world.

Thinking much about Jesus, as it happens I have seen from time to time a particular face which, as I look at it, I take to be his. It has come before me both sleeping and waking, and with such extraordinary clarity that I should surely recognize it instantly anywhere. Indeed, I quite often find myself searching for it among portraits – for instance, in the Prado Museum in Madrid, where, perhaps because of the superb display of paintings by El Greco, I found myself being especially vigilant – or about the streets, wherever the human countenance is on display. If I were an artist I believe I could paint or model it from memory, so familiar am I with its lineaments. To describe it in words is more difficult, as I have found when I have tried; the adjectives pile up, but fail to give the living, the total impression. If, for instance, I say that the face is reflective and passive rather than animated – which is the case – this at once suggests a lack of vivacity, whereas, in point of fact, the face is superlatively alive. Again, this very aliveness is not just animation, but a quality which characterizes and suffuses all perfection; in art or in creatures, in Michelangelo's *Risen Christ* as in Blake's tyger burning bright. A swarthy, rather heavy-featured face, with large, dark, glowing eyes, not by any means mild in the conventional sense, but rather formidable, powerful; explaining why, at his words, the money-changers scattered, and Lazarus rose from the dead, why the crowds listened to him as to one having authority. A calm, serious, strong, beautiful face, whose inherent sensuality has been diffused into love which shines out of it like light. If I ever set eyes on the face, in this world or the next, it will be for me a moment of great and joyous recognition.

Jesus himself was insistent that what he had to say would be more comprehensible to the simple than to the sophisticated, and that to understand him it was necessary to become like a little child. To see God – the essential purpose of living at all – was the prerogative of the pure of heart. *I thank thee, O Father, Lord of Heaven and earth,* the Gospels quote Jesus as praying, *that thou didst hide these things from the wise and understanding, and didst reveal them unto babes.* In accordance with this conviction, his first disciples were fishermen, who, though they may well have been relatively prosperous, to the point of being employers of labour, were certainly not, other than in a very primitive sense, educated, or even literate. An exception was perhaps Judas Iscariot, who must at any rate have been able to keep accounts, because he was in charge of their common store of money. The objection he raised to pouring expensive spikenard ointment over Jesus's head, that the money it cost would have been better distributed to the poor, reads very like a short leader in the *Guardian* animadverting upon the good works that might be financed by selling off the Vatican's treasures. It is the poor and simple who delight in the extravagances of love and liturgy; only rich Quakers can afford to worship austerely. Again, Judas betrayed Jesus with a kiss, which somehow has about it a flavour of sophistication and dreaming spires, of Swinburne's pale Galilean and Rupert Brooke's magnificent unpreparedness for the long littleness of life. If Peter had betrayed Jesus, he would just have pointed, and then fled in shame.

So, a carpenter's shop in Nazareth rather than a liberal education in Rome or Athens, followed by a conducted tour of the pagan world, was the requisite preparation for Jesus's ministry; as was belonging to a rebellious subject people like the Jews, which enabled him to understand the nature and workings of power in a way that would have been impossible if God had chosen to become incarnate in the person of, say, a Roman senator. He needed to experience at first hand the hazards and ardours of earning a living in order to be able to teach us with conviction to pray: *Give us this day our daily bread* — seven words singularly beautiful and touching, and calculated to explode all the fantasies of affluence, and convey the basic condition of our existence, which is still, at any rate for the great majority of mankind, that to have the wherewithal to get through a day represents the limit of human aspiration. Similarly, Jesus needed to belong to a subject people to know and understand, in the words of the *Magnificat*, that the mighty, whoever they may be, are fated to be put down from their seats, and the humble and meek to be exalted in their place; who then become mighty in their turn, and so fit to be put down. Only the oppressed can understand oppression, as only the poor can understand poverty. Hence it is that, of all the accounts of twentieth-century oppression — probably the most appalling ever because of the moral vacuity of the oppressors, and the monstrous resources which technology and medicine have put at their disposal — Solzhenitsyn's is the best and most authentic. *One Day in the Life of Ivan Denisovich, The First Circle* and *The Gulag Archipelago* are written out of his own suffering, which, as with Tolstoy, led to his becoming a Christian.

Because Jesus possessed nothing, he could dare to say: *Blessed be ye poor*; because he had no status, national or social, he could call to him *all ye that labour and are heavy laden*, and promise, *I will give*

you rest. Simone Weil describes how one evening when she was feeling very wretched she visited a little Portuguese village by the sea on the day of its patronal festival. There was a full moon, and the wives of the fishermen were going in procession from ship to ship, carrying candles and singing ancient hymns of a heart-rending sadness. As she listened to them, her own sadness lifted, and she suddenly had a joyous conviction 'that Christianity is pre-eminently the religion of slaves, that slaves cannot help belonging to it, and I among others'. I have been similarly uplifted when, gloomily pacing the streets, or emerging from a restaurant or a shop or a television studio, a Christian face has met mine, smiling, a hand extended – young or old, bent or straight, black or white, I scarcely notice. Jesus's poverty and nonentity are credentials for becoming members of the Worshipful Company of Slaves. If he had been the Messiah of Jewish dreams, another King David leading his people to renewed national glory and independence, there never would have been a Christian religion; only yet another seeker after power through violence rather than salvation through love, proclaiming: Blessed are the enraged, for they shall subdue the earth; Blessed they who do hunger and thirst after vengeance, for they shall be revenged; Blessed the impure of heart, for they shall be spared the sight of God.

Jesus first emerges into the public eye when he appears among those seeking baptism from John the Baptist. He was now, we are told, a grown man, round about thirty years old, with, it must be assumed, a formed character and disposition. If, as seems likely, Joseph had by this time died – he makes no further appearance in the Gospels – then, as the eldest son, Jesus must have been responsible for keeping the Nazareth home together and looking after his numerous stepbrothers and stepsisters. After his baptism and entering upon his ministry, he rejected family ties, and even spoke slightingly of them – an attitude which may have been intensified by a move on the part of his relatives to have him put away as being out of his mind. In view of the, as they must have seemed, wild claims he was making, and the strange stories circulating about him, such a move would not have been entirely untoward. Throughout history, truth has been considered a form of dementia, and those who have turned away from fantasy and fixed their eyes on reality, judged insane. When Jesus said that *whosoever shall do the will of God, the same is my brother, and my sister and mother*, he meant simply that now, for the short time remaining to him, his mission was everything, his personal life nothing. In the great saints and teachers there is this strange, and at times forbidding, impersonality; 'I see little of Mr Blake nowadays,'

Blake's wife, Catherine, said of him towards the end of his life; 'he spends so much of his time in heaven.' Blake, too, was considered mad, even by most of his admirers; nowadays, drugs and psychiatry would make short work of him – of Jesus, too, for that matter.

The preaching of John the Baptist had been making a considerable stir, the more so because, with his ascetic way of life in the desert, his diet of locusts and wild honey, his bizarre clothing of camel's hair held together by a leather belt about his waist, he conformed closely to the style of the Hebrew prophets of old. Indeed, many thought he was Elijah reincarnated – a view Jesus himself appears to have held at one point. The description of him as *a burning and shining light*, as *the voice of one crying in the wilderness, Make straight the way of the Lord*, fitted in with Scriptural prophecies; as did his proclamation of God's kingdom, and the forthcoming fulfilment of Messianic hopes. The public response was so great that word of it even reached Josephus; people crowded to the River Jordan to listen to John and he baptized in readiness for the new age that was upon them. In his preaching John was insistent that he was no more than a precursor announcing the coming of one mightier than he the latchet of whose shoes he was not worthy to unloose. The Law, he said, was given by Moses, but this other one, this Servant of the Lord whose coming was announced by Isaiah, would bring grace and truth. When he saw Jesus coming with the others for baptism, he at once recognized him, and shouted out: *Behold the Lamb of God, which taketh away the sin of the world!*

In this encounter between Jesus and John the Baptist by the River Jordan the New Testament confronted the Old, John being the last spokesman of the dispensation of Moses, and Jesus the inaugurator of a new dispensation of redemption which was to replace it. John first declines to baptize Jesus; it should, he insists, be the other way round, he soliciting Jesus for baptism. Jesus, however, will not be persuaded; now it must be this way round, later perhaps otherwise. So John accedes to his wish, and Jesus is baptized. All the Gospels agree that when this happened the heavens were opened, and the Holy Ghost descended in the bodily shape of a dove, and a voice was heard coming from heaven and saying: *This is my beloved Son, in whom I am well pleased.* To a twentieth-century mind any suggestion that such happenings actually occurred is preposterous. If the heavens seemed to open, it will have been a natural break in the clouds; if a dove descended upon Jesus, it just happened to be flying in that direction; if a voice was heard from on high, it was surely imagined, or came from some bystander. At the best, the word 'symbolism' will be used by way of explanation. If it had been a matter of pre-historic bones – even palpably fraudulent ones like the Piltdown Man – then credulity would have been plentifully forthcoming. Each age devises and believes its own fantasies. In any case, whatever may or may not have happened, Jesus's baptism was a great turning-point in his life on earth, when he realized with perfect clarity and precision that what was required of him was no less than to make known to men the ways and purposes of God. There are such moments in life; when a truth crystallizes, from being implicit becoming explicit, and all creation seems to participate – the sun shining more warmly, the air breathed in more exhilaratingly, the grass greener, the trees taller and the flowers brighter. The addition of clouds opening, a dove descending, a voice speaking, is not, after all, in the circumstances so very out of the way.

Jesus's baptism, then, was the beginning of his ministry; the moment when his destiny settled upon him. Whatever domestic duties he was still involved in automatically came to an end; whatever plans or expectations he might have in his mortal capacity must now be relinquished. He was now God's Son indeed, and only concerned to go about his Father's business. Doubtless, too, at that moment a premonition came to him of the inevitable end. The Messiah had been announced and acclaimed by John the Baptist, but in a guise which could not but be abhorrent to those who most ardently awaited him – not riding clouds of glory, but a borrowed donkey; not breathing fire against Israel's enemies, but calling on all men to love one another; not restoring a Jewish throne, but scorning all thrones except only God's heavenly one. What was there to do with such a Messiah but kill him? For John, too, the baptism of Jesus was climacteric. The Lord whose coming he had prophesied had now come; his own role, as far as the Gospels were concerned, was finished. We hear vaguely of his troubles with Herod, and then of his tragic end; but in the unfolding of the drama of Jesus's life he had no further part to play. Even after his death he continued to have followers, as we read in the Acts of the Apostles; and there is an echo of his extreme asceticism and fiery words in the fascinating account of the Essenes at Qumran which came to light in the Dead Sea Scrolls; though it is extremely improbable that John ever joined the Qumran community, and quite inconceivable that Jesus did, as has been suggested. John and the Essenes, in any case, were specifically Jewish; Jesus belongs to all mankind.

Why, one may wonder, did Jesus choose to be baptized at all? What need was there for him to follow John's behest and repent in preparation for the coming of his own kingdom? Furthermore, what had Jesus to repent of, being sinless? This is like asking why the Word needed to become flesh in the first place; why it did not suffice just as Word. The point is that, to exist for us in time, the Word had to be spoken, and that the Incarnation was God's way of speaking it. Or, as it is put in the Fourth Gospel, in becoming flesh in the person of Jesus, the Word *dwelt among us*. Thus, though Jesus's coming into the world was divinely ordained, and represented God's deliberate intervention in history, it was still the case that he had to live in the world as a man among other men. In this capacity, he heard and heeded John's call to repentance and accepted baptism at John's hands, just as, later, he accepted crucifixion at Pilate's. In this capacity, too, he understood, fully and perfectly, the nature and driving force of sin. How otherwise could he have insisted that just to look after a woman to lust after her is to commit adultery? This is sinner's knowledge, as all sinners at once recognize. How otherwise could he know that the insatiable ego ever raising its cobra head will not be coaxed or persuaded or indulged into quiescence, but must be struck down once and for all? That to live we must die, experiencing the ultimate sweetness of life, the final fragrance and music of it, only in its final rejection? That when at last we know that life is worthless, then only do we truly live; that when we have absolutely nothing more to hope for – no dream, however exalted, of delighting or uplifting our fellows, no vista of fulfilled love or of silver evening light falling serenely across our last days – then, at last, we can hope? That when the heart is empty, the mind dry, the soul blown away in dust, and the sheet of white paper that has to be covered stares back at us glassy-eyed, then, and only then, a flame leaps up of certainty, absolute and everlasting, that God awaits us with outstretched arms to welcome us into the eternity whence we came? This is what Jesus knew – sinners' knowledge, garnered in sinlessness.

After his baptism by John the Baptist, Jesus, the Gospels relate, withdrew into the desert to fast and meditate for forty days and forty nights – doubtless corresponding to the forty years the Children of Israel spent wandering in the desert on their way from Egypt to the Promised Land. St Paul similarly withdrew into the desert after his Damascus Road experience, when from being a persecutor of the Christians he became their most brilliant and audacious spokesman and champion throughout the pagan world. It is a natural impulse thus to seek isolation and quiet after an experience which dramatically reshapes and redirects a life, like the crystallization in Jesus's mind of what God expected of him. It was during his time in the desert, we are told, that Jesus encountered the Devil, who made various tempting propositions to him.

Even those who are prepared in a vague way to acknowledge the existence of a deity draw the line at the Devil. A Creator of the universe and planner of its and our destinies who wound up the evolutionary process in the first place and then left it to unwind itself – yes, just conceivable; but a Devil representing the contrary principle, destructive rather than creative, malevolent rather than beneficent, is another matter, and quite out of the question. Personally, I have found the Devil easier to believe in than God; for one thing, alas, I have had more to do with him. It seems to me quite extraordinary that anyone should have failed to notice, especially during the last half century, a diabolic presence in the world, pulling downwards as gravity does instead of pressing upwards as trees and plants do when they grow and reach so resolutely and beautifully after the light. A counter-force to creativity; destructive in its nature and purpose, raging far and wide like a forest fire, and burning in the heart's core – pinpointed there, a fiery tongue of fierce desire. Have we not seen this Devil's destructiveness making a bonfire of past, present and future in one mighty conflagration? Smelt him, rancid-sweet? Touched him, slippery-soft? Measured with the eye his fearful shape. Heard his fearful rhetoric? Glimpsed him, sometimes in a mirror, with drooling, greedy mouth, misty ravening eyes and flushed flesh? Who can miss him in those blackest of all moments, when God seems to have disappeared, leaving the Devil to occupy an empty universe?

Reconstructing Jesus's encounter with the Devil, for the purpose of filming it, presented difficulties. The location was easy enough – anywhere in the stretch of desert between Jerusalem and the Dead Sea. The time, too – at that dramatic moment, when the shadows are longest and jackal cries shrillest: just before the sun sinks below the horizon, to go out like a light, leaving the burning sand suddenly cold and dead. The difficulty was the Devil's appearance. How should we show him? Should he be portrayed as a combination of a company-promoter with several bankruptcies behind him, a leader-writer on a soon-to-be-defunct liberal newspaper, and a lapsed Jesuit? Something between Don Quixote and Frank Harris, with a touch of a moustached life-peeress easy on marijuana. Finally, it was decided that the Devil's presence should be conveyed only by a long dark shadow falling across the sand, and lengthening as the colloquy with Jesus proceeded. It may even have been Jesus's own shadow; dialogues with the Devil have a way of turning out to be soliloquies.

What the Devil wanted of Jesus, as Dostoevsky brings out so brilliantly in the confrontation between the Grand Inquisitor and the returned Christ in *The Brothers Karamazov*, was, essentially, to involve him in the exigencies of power, thereby neutralizing his gospel of love, and leaving mankind still at the Devil's mercy. Jesus represents the only serious adversary the Devil has to reckon with, so naturally he rates special attention. In this assault on Jesus the Devil began with bread, calculating that after his fasting Jesus would be hungry, and that anyway, with his deeply compassionate nature, he could not but feel for the hungry everywhere, who then, as now, abounded. So, the Devil whispered, why not use his miraculous powers to turn stones into bread? Not just for himself, of course, though in point of fact he could do with a bite, but to feed the hungry whoever and wherever they might be. What a benefactor that would make of Jesus! How it would glorify his name thus to respond to the improvidence and selfishness of men by drawing, as he could, on the profligacy of God, to His greater glory!

Curiously enough, just at the right moment to begin filming, when the shadows were long enough and the light not too weak, I happened to notice near by a whole expanse of stones, all identical, and looking uncommonly like loaves, well baked and brown. How easy for Jesus to have turned these stone loaves into edible ones, as, later, he would turn water into wine at a wedding feast! And, after all, why not? The Roman authorities distributed free bread to promote Caesar's kingdom, and Jesus could do the same to promote his. Altogether, the Devil's offer was cleverly devised to be alluring, as his offers always are. On consideration, though, Jesus saw through it, and turned it down. Free bread might advance the cult of Caesar in any of its versions, then or thereafter; but, as Jesus told the Devil, *Man shall not live by bread alone, but by every word that proceedeth out of the mouth of God.* His physical requirements are secondary to his spiritual ones, and if he seeks even so basic a necessity as bread as an end, it can only result in his spiritual starvation.

Jesus returns to this theme again and again, promising those who would follow him the bread of life, which, unlike mere eating bread, would satisfy their hunger for ever. At the Last Supper, too, which was also the first Eucharist, he drew a comparison between the bread they were eating and the body he would shortly offer as a sacrifice for them and all mankind; and it was when he broke bread that his two companions on the Road to Emmaus recognized him as their Saviour. Bread, in his estimation, was to the body what the truth he proclaimed was to the soul. It had its own sanctity, and just for that reason could

And when the tempter came to him, he said, If thou be the Son of God, command that these stones be made bread.

DETAIL OF STAINED-GLASS WINDOW FROM TROYES CATHEDRAL

52

not be procured, as the Devil proposed, miraculously from stones. Jesus never thus used his miraculous powers to promote any general or collective purpose. The salvation he offered was for individuals, not collectivities; for a person, not for an idea. Though the sick crowded round him, there were no collective cures or blanket dispensations. On one occasion, it is true, feeling compassion for a large crowd which had long been listening to him, and must, he felt, have grown hungry, he managed to make a few loaves and fishes stretch to meeting their needs. This, like the Eucharistic ritual, may well have been a token meal, symbolizing the spiritual refreshment they had been receiving. Or, more probably, as I like to think, the loaves and fishes were refreshments which one person had prudently brought, and then, under the inspiration of Jesus's teaching, offered to help meet the general need; whereupon others followed suit, so that it turned out there was plenty for everyone, and even some basketsful to spare. If this was indeed so, it was a greater miracle than merely multiplying the original loaves and fishes would have been. Admittedly, we who are familiar with Jesus's words seem to manage without undue unease to eat when others go hungry; but surely, hearing him actually speak the words would have induced us to look up, at any rate momentarily, from our own particular trough.

The Devil's second proposition to Jesus was that he should use his miraculous powers to draw attention to himself and his cause. What he needed to get his message across was to be spot-lighted; to get into the news and become a celebrity. After all, the Devil's argument ran, words of truth such as Jesus spoke were all very well, but what if they were ignored, or, worse, induced anger and hostility? What if people who sat in darkness and saw his great light actually preferred the darkness? Now marvels would catch and hold their attention. Supposing, then, Jesus were to hurl himself from one of the Temple's high pinnacles in the sure knowledge that God would send His angels to ensure that no ill befell him. What a sensation that would make! Headlines in all the papers, stories on all the television networks, everyone making for Jerusalem to interview the Man Who Jumped off the Top of the Temple Without Hurting Himself. Jesus in great demand everywhere; a ready-made international audience hanging on his words; Herod interested, Pilate, too, and maybe the Emperor Tiberias himself. All this not to boost Jesus – not at all, but to ensure that his words resounded through the great Roman Empire rather than just reaching a rag-tag and bob-tail following in Galilee.

We who have lived in an age of technological marvels can easily understand this effort of persuasion on the Devil's part. Taking a

55

leaf out of the Devil's book, governments try to dazzle us and make themselves acceptable by arranging visits to the moon and other wonders; advertisers, likewise, by means of miraculous visual images, demonstrate the delectable consequences that will follow smoking such a cigarette, visiting such a resort, anointing ourselves with such an unguent or swallowing such a potion. So many and such diverse marvels, offered on the Devil's behalf, find a multitude of takers; but Jesus knew better, and kept his head. His particular relationship with God, and God's care of him, were part of God's concern for all creation, extending, Jesus was to tell us, even to a sparrow falling to the ground. Just because of this, God's concern for him was not to be put to the test and exploited as the Devil proposed. *Thou shalt not tempt the Lord thy God*, he quoted from the Scriptures in rebuffing the Devil for the second time; God's love for Jesus and His love for a sparrow were part of the same universal love which shines through all His creation, and must no more be particularized than a mother's love for one of her children over another.

It was this very universality of God's love and compassion, falling like rain on the just and unjust, on the virtuous and sinners, on sparrows and men and the Son of Man, that Jesus came into the world to proclaim, contrasting it with the preoccupation of particular deities with particular people, places and interests. If he had fallen in with the Devil's proposal to publicize himself he would have reduced what was destined to become a universal religion to the dimensions of a cult.

For the same reason, he poured scorn on all requests, even from his disciples, for a sign from Heaven. A sign was too easy; what Jesus asked for was faith, whereby mountains could be moved, and the blind could be made to see, the infirm to rise up and to walk and the dead to come alive. The only worthwhile sign, Jesus insisted, was the truth of what he had to say. No other was needed or appropriate. Thus, when, under his questioning, the disciples admitted that they considered Jesus to be the promised Messiah and Son of God, he begged them to keep the thought strictly to themselves. Again, at the Transfiguration, when Jesus's face shone with the mystical light of one who had drawn close to God, he gave the three disciples who were with him strict instructions that they should mention what they had seen to no one. On another occasion, he gently rebuked a young man who had addressed him as *Good Master* with: *Why callest thou me good? None is good, save one, that is, God*. In other words, while he was incarnate he insisted on being regarded in every respect as a mortal man. Had he done otherwise, the focus and climax of all his teaching, the Cross, would have lost its point. For a man to die on a Cross for other men was sublime, whereas for God to be crucified would be nothing – like someone who is immortal serving a prison sentence. Thus, if the Devil had succeeded in persuading Jesus to exploit his miraculous powers to his own greater glory in the eyes of the world, his mission would have been emptied of its content. To fulfil his mission he had to accept all the limitations, fallibilities and inadequacies of our mortal existence and relate these to our immortal destiny, thereby enabling men to draw near to God, and God to make Himself accessible to men.

The last of the Devil's propositions was the widest sweeping of all. This time he took Jesus to the top of a high mountain from which all the kingdoms of the world could be seen. There, the Devil explained that the kingdoms were in his gift, and Jesus could have them, to do what he liked with them. All that would be required of him in return was to bow down and worship the Devil instead of God. Without a doubt, the offer was perfectly valid, and made, in Devilish terms, in good faith. As the mainspring of power and the true manipulator of the human will, the Devil had, and has, the kingdoms of the earth at his disposition, to enthrone and dethrone whom he will. Jesus had but to give a nod of agreement and he could have constructed Christendom, not on four shaky Gospels and a defeated man nailed on a Cross, but on a basis of sound socio-economic planning and principles. He could have instituted welfare states *in excelsis*, with all human requirements, from birth pills to cremation, made available gratis to one and all; set in train arrangements whereby happiness was not just pursued, but caught and captured, for the pursuer to have and to hold till death did them part; triumphantly installed the proletariat of the world in power on the best Marxist lines, and seen to it that government duly withered away, leaving mankind to live happily ever after. Every utopia could have been brought to pass, every hope have been realized and every dream been made to come true. What a benefactor, then, Jesus would have been! Acclaimed, equally, in the London School of Economics and the Harvard Business School; a statue in Parliament Square, and an even bigger one on Capitol Hill and in the Red Square; his picture carried, along with Lenin's and Marx's, on celebratory occasions in Moscow and Peking, and referred to approvingly in *Pravda*, *The Times*, the *Wall Street Journal* and the *Osservatore Romano*. Instead, he turned the offer down on the ground that only God should be worshipped. Thus a golden opportunity to establish a continuing city here and now, rather than going on seeking one to come, was lost for ever.

Or so it seemed. The Devil, however, is very patient, and knows how to wait. The offers that Jesus turned down found many takers among his ostensible representatives on earth, who, before many years had passed, were having themselves crowned on his behalf, going on Crusades to glorify his name, and generally managing in a variety of ingenious ways to turn his sayings round to have the exactly opposite meaning to what was intended. Our twentieth century, in this respect, has been a particularly fruitful time for the Devil, who has managed, among other remarkable feats, to launch Jesus as a fully-fledged freedom-fighter and urban guerrilla, with his Sermon on the Mount renamed the Sermon on the Barricades. Also to establish him as a champion of situational ethics for whom the flesh lusts with the spirit and the spirit with the flesh, so that we can do whatever we have a mind to.

This triumph lay ahead in a remote future, and when Jesus returned from the wilderness he left a discomfited Devil there. For him, it had been a time of great clarification; now he was absolutely sure about his vocation. In one of his parables he speaks about how *no man can enter into a strong man's house and spoil his goods, except he will first bind the strong man; and then he will spoil his house.* Was he perhaps here thinking of how, in the wilderness, he had, metaphorically speaking, bound the Devil in order to be able to put the Devil's kingdom of power out of the way before proclaiming to the world his own kingdom of love? After his colloquy with the Devil it was to be abundantly clear to him that always and in all circumstances he must eschew the three pillars of earthly authority – marvels, affluence and the exercise of power. It was not for him to turn stones into bread, however plentiful the stones and scarce the bread, but rather to sacramentalize bodily into spiritual sustenance; not for him to draw men to him by calling on God for a sign, but rather to light with his truth their way to God and God's way to them. Above all, it was not for him to look for help or support to any Caesar, actual or aspiring; still less to become one. He was to be no Führer, no mythical Resistance leader; there was poetry, but no rhetoric, in the words wherewith he would reveal to men how God would have them live together and do His will. The passionate Jewish nationalism which burned in John the Baptist's veins, and played so important a role in the Qumran Community, in so far as it ever meant anything to Jesus, was left behind in the wilderness with the Devil. His last act in company with his disciples before his Crucifixion was to wash their feet, as his last public appearance was in the accoutrements of a ribald King of the Jews – the former being an example of conduct unbecoming a Devil and a gentleman; the latter, conduct disgracing the Devil's uniform.

With these points thus clarified, Jesus could take up his role as the Messiah whose coming had been foretold, and embark upon his ministry. Everything was to be exactly as prophesied, except that it would be in reverse – a looking-glass Messiahship of the defeated. As one man, Adam, had estranged men from God, so another man, Jesus, would reconcile them to God; as Adam's disobedience necessitated Moses's Law, so Jesus's obedience opened up a new dispensation of love transcending Moses's Law in relations between man and man, and between men and God. It was a way of putting things that, for obvious reasons, appealed to Jews; but even today, when Adam is considered to have disappeared without trace on Darwin's *Voyage of the Beagle*, the symbolism stands. Jesus's sacrifice undoes Adam's sin; the Old Man with his deeds is put off, and the New Man, reborn in the spirit, put on; and all mankind, Jew and gentile, bond and free, can join together in one body, in one fellowship, with, and in, Christ. This was the new heaven and the new earth prophesied in the Scriptures; but to be realized, Jesus was to insist, in humility, not vainglory, in sacrifice, not triumph, in affliction, not material wellbeing.

As the long, ardently and patiently awaited Messiah, then, Jesus would offer his followers, not the exhilaration of power, but the ecstasy of love, inviting them to share with him in the public ridicule and obloquy, and, ultimately, in the rage and abhorrence, which so strange an interpretation of his Messianic role must inevitably arouse, alike in the Sanhedrin and among Resistance zealots. His way, as he was aware from the beginning, could have only one destination; and the final paradox of his ministry was to make of that destination – himself on a Cross between two others – the symbol and the focus of the wildest and most audacious hopes ever to be entertained in the human heart. Meanwhile, he must set about fulfilling his mission without delay. Time was pressing; as he was to put it to his disciples, using one of his beautiful images: *Say not ye, There are yet four months, and then cometh harvest? behold, I say unto you, Lift up your eyes, and look on the fields; for they are white already to harvest.* Going about in Galilee and teaching in the synagogues, he made a great impression on all who heard him, until he came to the synagogue in Nazareth, where he had lived with his family. He began by repeating a magnificent passage from the prophet Isaiah: *The Spirit of the Lord is upon me, because he hath anointed me to preach the gospel to the poor; he hath sent me to heal the brokenhearted, to preach deliverance to the captives, and recovering of sight to the blind, to set at liberty them that are bruised, to preach the acceptable year of the Lord.*

It was the dream of all the prophets – the hope of every wellwisher of the human race from the beginning of time; of Bunyan's Pilgrim as of Cervantes's Knight of the Woeful Countenance; of every utopian and *exalté* up to, and including, especially, our own time – to bring good news to the poor and the afflicted, to restore sight to the blind and liberty to the captive, to enable mankind to live together in peace and love. Assuredly, Jesus will have delivered the passage with great feeling and conviction; equally surely, the congregation were deeply impressed. It was only when he began to extemporize and particularize that doubts set in; then dismay, and then fury. For Jesus boldly announced that the fulfilment of the Scripture he had quoted was not in some remote future, but then and there, and in the person of the one who was speaking to them. He, Jesus, had been anointed to preach the acceptable year of the Lord. It was now upon them, and it behoved them to respond by repenting of their sins and putting aside their worldly preoccupations to make themselves worthy of the destiny God had prepared for them. This was what he had to say, and was to go on saying, until his arrest and execution. In Nazareth it was too much for them. Was not this fantastic claim being made by someone they knew, whose family they knew – the carpenter, Joseph's son. How could he be the promised Messiah, who was to come in glory at the end of the days and restore Israel's glory? It was absurd, and he must be mad. They threw him out of the synagogue, and then, continuing to pursue him with threats and abuse, thought to silence him for ever by pushing him over the edge of the hill on which Nazareth is built – a place easily discernible today. Somehow Jesus evaded them and went his way. His hour had not yet come; the drama was only at its beginning. He made for Capernaum to continue his ministry.

PART 2

What Jesus Came To Tell The World

There are particular moments in the lives of men and in the history of mankind when what is permanently true (if largely unrecognized) becomes manifestly and effectively true. Such a moment in history is reflected in the Gospels. The presence of God with men, a truth for all times and places, becomes an effective truth. It became such (we must conclude) because of the impact Jesus made; because in his words and actions it was presented with exceptional clarity and operative with exceptional power. Jesus himself pointed to the effects of his work as signs of the coming of the kingdom: *If by the finger of God I drive out devils, then be sure the Kingdom of God has come upon you.*

C. H. DODD

Jesus's good news, then, was that the Kingdom of God had come, and that he, Jesus, was its herald and expounder to men. More than that, in some special, mysterious way, he *was* the Kingdom. The history of the Children of Israel, God's chosen people, was now focused in one single individual, himself, and would reach its final fulfilment through, and in, him. Thus Jesus could, without blasphemy, speak for God, who in a quite particular sense was his Father. Furthermore, no one – a breath-taking claim – could approach the Father save through him; his words were the Father's, making clear to men how God wished them to live, what values should govern their lives and their relations with Him and with one another. Jesus and the Father, that is to say, were one; to reject Jesus, as the prophets had been rejected, would amount to rejecting God himself.

As C. S. Lewis has truly pointed out, such statements rule out completely any notion that Jesus was merely a superlatively good man – a belief in which I was brought up, but which seemed to me even as a child singularly flaccid and unconvincing. It made Jesus a sort of super-Emerson or proletarian Marcus Aurelius, but took no account of the drama in which he was the central figure. And it was this drama that, even before I could understand it, held my fascinated attention. 'A man who was merely a man and said the sort of things

61

Jesus said', Lewis writes, 'would not be a great moral teacher. He would either be a lunatic – on a level with the man who says he is a poached egg – or else he would be the Devil of Hell. You must make your choice.' Lewis was right: we have to make this choice, recognizing that Jesus was either, as he claimed, the Son of God, or a megalomaniac to the point of being demented, and, consciously or unconsciously, a fraud. 'You can shut him up for a fool', Lewis goes on; 'you can spit at him and kill him as a demon; or you can fall at his feet and call him Lord and God. But let us not come with any patronizing nonsense about his being a great human teacher. He has not left that open to us. He did not intend to.'

Jesus's talk of being on intimate terms with God and His appointed spokesman on earth, understandably enough, was blasphemy in the ears of the Sanhedrin, and especially of the High Priest, Caiaphas; and it may be doubted whether even the disciples, who were constantly in Jesus's company, fully understood what was signified. Certainly, casual listeners will have been mystified. To help them – and us – to understand, Jesus produced one of his parables. His special genius as a teacher and communicator lay in these parables, which were vivid little stories, each one complete in itself. Being in the idiom and imagery of everyday life, they were easily and immediately comprehensible, and held the attention of simple, unlettered people as mystical or intellectual themes never would have done. Read now, they give one the feel, as nothing else does, of what life was like for Jesus two thousand years ago; how he reacted to things and people, what caught his eye and interested him. No one can fail to be aware of the teller; behind the parables one senses a perceptive, often ironic, brilliantly creative mind. Unmistakably, they are the work of an artist rather than of a thinker, or, in the narrower meaning of the word, moralist.

A measure of their artistry is the clumsiness and laboriousness of efforts made to interpret them. There have been some truly astonishing performances in this field, of which St Augustine provided a prize example in his interpretation of the parable of the Good Samaritan. Jericho, he tells us, meant the moon, and signifies our mortality, because it is born, waxes, wanes and dies. The thieves are the Devil and his angels, who strip the traveller of his immortality, beat him by persuading him to sin, and leave him half-dead in that, knowing God, he is alive, and, having sinned, he is dead, and so in a half-in-half condition between life and death. So it goes on and on, concluding that the two pence the Samaritan (meaning guardian and therefore Jesus himself) left with the innkeeper (St Paul) are either

the two precepts of love, or the promise of this life and of that which
is to come. Poor Augustine! He must have thought he was back in
his Chair of Rhetoric elucidating a text for dim-witted students.

The parable Jesus devised to proclaim the coming of the Kingdom,
and his own part in it, is about an absentee landlord who lets off his
vineyard to husbandmen or tenant cultivators. The arrangement is
that they should pay their rent in kind in the form of a proportion of
the produce. So far so good; but when the landlord sends underlings
to collect the produce due, the cultivators, instead of fulfilling the
bargain they have made, beat up the landlord's men and drive them
away. Such happenings were, it appears, fairly common in Galilee

63

in Jesus's time, the country being still unpacified after an abortive rising in AD 6. It was common for large estates to be owned by absentee foreigners, who let them out to tenant cultivators, just as the landlord in Jesus's parable did. If the tenants then reneged on meeting their obligations to their landlord, even to the point of rough-handling his agents, public sympathy was liable to be with them, as it was, for instance, in Ireland in comparable circumstances during the Troubles which preceded national independence. The landlord in the parable finally decides to send his son to collect what is due to him, calculating that surely the tenants will treat him with respect. On the contrary, they do not just beat up the son, as they have the other emissaries, but they murder him, thereby disposing of the heir, and grabbing the property for themselves. What, the parable concludes, might the owner of the vineyard be expected to do in such a case? Surely, to come in person to destroy the cultivators and hand over the vineyard to others.

When Jesus told the parable, his own fate was unknown, at least to his listeners; but the members of the early Church for whom the Gospels were written would have found no difficulty in grasping that the landlord was God, and his vineyard, Israel, whose rulers, the tenant cultivators, had indeed rejected and persecuted God's emissaries, and then, when His son was sent among them, engineered his Crucifixion. By AD 70, they would have known, too, that retribution followed in the form of the destruction of the Temple and the dispersal of the Jews, and would have easily persuaded themselves that they, for the most part converted Gentiles, were the new tenants, who might be relied on punctually to fulfil their obligations to their landlord, *rendering him the fruits in their seasons*. No doubt, the parable is somewhat angled in the Gospels to fit in with this shape of events; but as Jesus told it originally, its essential meaning will have been clear. The Messiah of prophecy was for the Jews exclusively, and his Kingdom an Israel restored to greatness and glory; the Messiah in the person of Jesus is not for a Chosen People, but for all who will accept him, and his Kingdom is not of this world at all. It is, at once, within us, and located beyond the confines of space and time and mortality. We carry it about with us in our inner being, infinitely precious, as it might be some locket containing the likeness of a beloved face. At the same time, like Augustine's City of God, it is high above us, out of our reach – Isaiah's *land that is very far off*; but still, for those that have eyes to see, descernible from our earthly city and the destination of our earthly pilgrimage. It is both here and now, available to everyone for the asking, and to be vigilantly expected – as

64

the wise virgins awaited the coming of the bridegroom, with their lamps full of oil, unlike the foolish ones who had used up their oil, and then, when the bridegroom came, had no means of replenishing their lamps.

The single condition for entering into the Kingdom is to be reborn; as is explained in a very interesting and significant conversation Jesus had with one Nicodemus, described as *a man of the Pharisees . . . a ruler of the Jews* – in other words, an important personage who was required, by virtue of his position, to give an impression, in his dress and behaviour, of the strictest orthodoxy. Nicodemus, we are told, came to Jesus by night, obviously not wishing to be seen visiting him. Anyone who has associated himself with causes considered to be unfashionable or disreputable will be familiar with such nocturnal visitors of distinction who offer every sort of help and encouragement short of standing up to be counted. Reading between the lines of the account of Jesus's talk with Nicodemus as given in the Fourth Gospel, one can sense a certain asperity on Jesus's part, doubtless due to the hole-and-corner nature of Nicodemus's approach to him.

Nicodemus began with flattery, addressing Jesus as 'Rabbi', which coming from a Pharisee in conversation with a wayward and reputedly crazy evangelist from Galilee, was decidedly – putting it mildly – unusual. *We know,* he began, *that thou art a teacher come from God; for no man can do these miracles that thou doest, except God be with him.* It was a mistaken approach, especially the speaking on behalf of the Pharisees as a body, and making the miracles, rather than the truth of his words and the authority with which he spoke them, the sign that Jesus's mission was divinely ordained. This was precisely what he had scornfully rejected when the Devil suggested using his miraculous powers to validate his Messianic credentials. So, he just ignored what Nicodemus had said, and bluntly stated that *except a man be born again, he cannot see the kingdom of God.* Nicodemus responded by pretending to be a simpleton: *How can a man be born when he is old? Can he enter the second time into his mother's womb and be born?* To which Jesus answered that to enter into the Kingdom of God it is necessary first to be washed clean of past sins by baptism such as John the Baptist offered, and then to be born again spiritually; for *that which is born of the flesh is flesh; and that which is born of the Spirit is spirit.* So clever a man as Nicodemus, Jesus went on, really oughtn't to be surprised when told that he must be born anew; after all, *the wind bloweth where it listeth, and thou hearest the sound thereof, but canst not tell whence it cometh, and whither it goeth; so is everyone that is born of the Spirit.* In response to which Nicodemus could only mutter rather feebly: *How can these things be?* Then Jesus really let him have it. Nicodemus, a teacher of Israel, and he couldn't understand! Jesus and his followers spoke of what they knew, witnessed to what they had seen; but the clever Pharisees would not accept their testimony. If when he told them about earthly things they remained sceptical, how could they hope to grasp what he was getting at when he spoke of heavenly things? Alone the Son of Man, precisely because he had descended out of heaven, could speak with authority of heavenly things; wherefore, *as Moses lifted up the serpent in the wilderness, even so must the Son of Man be lifted up; that whosoever believeth in him should not perish, but have eternal life.*

At this point, Nicodemus seems to have fallen silent, whereupon Jesus is reported as treating him to a concise statement of what he conceived to be his Messianic mission. God, he said, so loved the world that He sent his only begotten Son into the world, in order that whoever believed in him and had faith in his mission should not perish but have eternal life. He was emphatically not sent to judge the world; rather that the world, through him, should be saved. Believers, by the nature of the case, were not judged, and those who did not believe, had been judged already by virtue of rejecting the Son of God. This was their judgment – that light had come into the world, and they preferred darkness, their works being evil. *For every one that doeth evil hateth the light, neither cometh to the light, lest his deeds should be reproved.* How Nicodemus reacted to these words – if, indeed, they were actually addressed to him – we do not know; but at the time of the Crucifixion he will surely have remembered what Jesus said about the Son of Man being lifted up like Moses's serpent. This may well have induced him to join Joseph of Arimathaea, as he did, in taking Jesus's body down from the Cross, anointing it with a mixture of myrrh and aloes, preparing it for burial, and then placing it in a new tomb near by where no one had previously been buried. Later, too, the words of their nocturnal conversation will have recurred to him as he observed how the growing band of Christians were veritably reborn, as Jesus had told him he must be. May even what St Paul, a sometime fellow Pharisee, wrote to the Christians in Corinth have come to his notice? – *If any man be in Christ, he is a new creature: old things are passed away; behold, all things are become new. . . . Behold, now is the accepted time; behold, now is the day of salvation.*

Nicodemus's puzzlement over the notion of grown-up people being reborn is understandable enough. As Shakespeare puts it in his famous seven stages of man, we come into the world as babies mewling and puking in our nurse's arms; then pass from childhood to youth, to mature manhood, until finally we peter out in second childishness and mere oblivion. Where in this process is there a place for being reborn? Yet it happens. Out of the dark womb of our own wilfulness and carnality some force of spiritual creativity can push us into another birth. We emerge into the same world we have grown accustomed to, to find it now made new; its colours shining and translucent, its shapes sharpened and wonderful in their grace, its men and women moving like angels, and all its creatures disclosing a beauty hitherto secret. So, seeing with new eyes, I see a new world; understanding with heart and mind and soul, truth breaks upon me, not as a thought or sensation or realization, but in one comprehensive enlightenment. As a child with its first yawn or smile measures up to Time, I, reborn, and become a child again, measure up to Eternity. Who can doubt that this is the everlasting life Jesus promised – what is eternal in life becoming manifest eternally; each joy for ever in its joyfulness, each woe likewise in its woefulness, and the two inextricably intertwined; in Blake's words, 'woven fine, a clothing for the soul divine'.

Jesus's Kingdom was neither a dream of an earthly paradise, or utopia; nor was it a Dante-like vision of Heaven where souls which had successfully weathered the trials and troubles of this world might live happily ever after. It offered salvation to men and women living in the world; holding out to them the possibility of a way of life on quite different terms from any hitherto envisaged. Tasting Eternity in Time; experiencing heavenly ecstasies while still walking the earth; carrying love, not just to the ultimate requirements of the Law, of morality, of human affections, but far, far beyond that – into the crazy extravagancies of God's love, which knows no limits; which is poured out indiscriminately on all His creation, flooding it all with beauty, and making all its sounds – the grunts, the cries, the songs, the screeches – somehow melodious, not to mention words, which fill and billow like a sail to His breath, and glow with His translucence. No imaginable earthly utopia could be in such dimensions as these, nor any mere vision of heaven convey a like audacity in hoping and aspiring. This was a new era in human history that was being ushered in; the pagan world had grown old and tired and bored, but Jesus had prepared the way for a new springtime. One senses it in the writings of St Paul, in those wonderful poetic passages of his – *Who shall separate us from the love of Christ? Shall tribulation, or distress, or persecution, or famine, or nakedness, or peril, or sword? . . . O the depth of the riches both of the wisdom and knowledge of God! How unsearchable are his judgments, and his ways past finding out! . . . Though I speak with the tongues of men and of angels, and have not charity, I am become as sounding brass, or a tinkling cymbal* – in which the dear crabbed old Evangelist to whom we owe so much broke into song, filled with joy and wonder at living for and in Christ in Nero's world.

The joy and wonder were to continue unabated through all the troubles and pitfalls that lay ahead. *In the world ye shall have tribulation: but be of good cheer: I have overcome the world* – how often I have said over to myself with feelings of inexpressible comfort these words Jesus spoke to his disciples, knowing that when the test came they would scatter and lose heart, and regret ever having been associated with him! Jesus had indeed overcome the world, and for ever; but not as a conqueror or demagogue, not by force or chicanery. He had overcome the world by revealing its true nature, its reality, contrasting with the layer upon layer of fantasy which the human ego is endlessly constructing out of itself, like a monstrous coral reef. The revelation was Jesus's good news, the Kingdom he came to proclaim. In its light, we may know ourselves to be displaced persons, who yet are given eyes, if we care to use them, capable of seeing, here on earth, all the contours and geography of our true habitat and dwelling-place-to-be. What, then, are tribulations in a world so gloriously overcome? Thus, St Augustine preaching to his flock in Hippo after hearing the news of the sack of Rome:

> You are surprised that the world is losing its grip? That the world is grown old and full of pressing tribulations? Do not hold on to the old man, the world; do not refuse to regain your youth in Christ, who says to you: The world is passing away, the world is losing its grip, the world is short of breath. Do not fear, thy youth shall be renewed as an eagle.

Faced with tribulations no less pressing, we may heed Augustine's words, finding them as apposite as when they were first spoken fifteen centuries ago.

Inevitably, the Kingdom Jesus proclaimed took on some of the imagery, and aroused some of the expectations, of traditional Jewish apocalypticism. Through the years of dispersal and servitude the dream had persisted of the coming of a Messiah, a Son of Man, a Servant of the Lord, who would overthrow the oppressors of the Children of Israel and make them, as God's Chosen People, masters of the world. In some of the prophecies of Isaiah this dream is given a poetic, and even spiritual, expression:

> *The people that walked in darkness*
> *have seen a great light;*
> *They that dwell in the land of the shadow of death,*
> *upon them hath the light shined. . . .*

For unto us a child is born,
  unto us a son is given:
And the government shall be upon his shoulder;
  And his name shall be called
Wonderful, Counsellor, the mighty God,
  The everlasting Father, the Prince of Peace.
Of the increase of his government and peace
  there shall be no end. . . .
He shall not judge after the sight of his eyes,
  neither reprove after the hearing of his ears:
But with righteousness shall he judge the poor,
  and reprove with equity for the meek of the earth. . . .
And righteousness shall be the girdle of his loins,
  and faithfulness the girdle of his reins.

In other less elevated prophetic utterances – for instance, Daniel's – the furious indignation of the humble and meek, yearning to put down the mighty from their seats and be exalted in their place, gives rise to a sort of Biblical Marxism. After all, Karl Marx himself was a Hebrew prophet of a kind. The concern of Jesus, and of the writers of the Gospels, that he should be seen as fulfilling the Messianic prophecies, necessarily gets him involved in these diverse dreams of the deliverance of the Jews, and the coming to pass of a millennium to be heralded by the appearance of the Messiah on earth.

What was Jesus's own attitude? There can be little doubt that he saw himself as the Messiah; certainly he was executed for refusing to deny that he had made this claim. On the other hand, he seems to have been secretive about it, and to have disliked hearing himself called Messiah – or Christ, which amounted to the same thing. In Caesarea Philippi Jesus asked his disciples point-blank who people said he was. Some, they said, took him to be John the Baptist come to life, others Elijah, yet others Jeremiah or one of the prophets. *But whom say ye that I am?*, Jesus insisted. *Thou art the Christ, the Son of the living God*, Peter answered. Jesus was delighted; *Blessed art thou*, he said to Peter; *for flesh and blood hath not revealed it unto thee, but my Father which is in Heaven*. It was on this occasion, we are told, that Jesus went on to tell Peter he was true to his name – a rock; *and upon this rock I will build my church; and the gates of hell shall not prevail against it*. In terms of history, few sayings attributed to Jesus have proved more portentous, for upon it is based the whole mystique of the Catholic Church as the unique repository of God's purposes on earth and instrument of effecting them, with Peter as the first Pope to whom *the keys of the kingdom of heaven* have been entrusted.

However authentic this particular saying of Jesus may be – and it is one that, if he did not actually say it, the first Church Fathers had the strongest possible inducement to put in his mouth – it is certainly true that, despite many abominations and setbacks, the Church *has* lasted for a phenomenal length of time – longer, certainly, than any comparable institution. Thus it may legitimately be said that the gates of Hell have not so far prevailed against it. An outsider might consider that just now the Church's future looks blacker than at any time in its history, if only because the forces of discord and destruction are working from within; the gates of Hell might almost seem to have been set up at the entrance to the Vatican and to open inwards. Yet the faithful would surely say that Jesus's undertaking to St Peter remains valid, and must for ever. For myself, I cannot imagine myself believing that any institution, however long-lived and sacerdotal in its origins, can be other than subject to decay and dissolution.

The quest for Jesus necessarily leads through the many mansions of his Church on earth. Crouching in wooden pews, kneeling on cold stone, staring up hopelessly at painted ceilings, lips receiving the chalice, tongue the wafer – the body and blood of Christ. Bowed down before a carved figure, listening to sonorous words of prayer – 'Dearly beloved brethren, I pray and beseech you. . . .' Billowing surplice, silken hood, lace and lawn, vestments glorious enough for a celestial Wizard of Oz; or, jowled and black suited, words soberly spoken – Father, we *do* ask thee. . . . Or maybe a mutton-chopped, youthful visage, ardently earnest, praying for peace between the nations, a juster distribution of the world's wealth, an end to colonial exploitation – trifles carelessly tossed, one after the other, into a pool of prayer. Little conventicles, majestic cathedrals, substantial chapels, street-corner bands, speakers with tongues, heavenly pop groups twanging for Jesus – like someone looking for a lost love; searching, peering, shouting through the echoing emptiness or into the swelling sound: 'Are you there? Oh, are you there?' Or eagerly questioning: 'Has he been this way? Are you expecting him? Will he come?' And the answer: 'He was here. . . . He may be coming. . . . He's expected. . . .' But never: 'Yes, he's here!' Never that! Through the many mansions, up and down the stairs, in and out of the folding doors, sweetest Plainsong sounding; shining faces, outstretched 'hands, welcoming smiles; organ notes booming, fragile words intoned or spoken. So many intimations, but never him, to fall at his feet. 'At last! Lord!'

In any case, Jesus did not come into the world to found a Church but to proclaim a Kingdom – the two being by no means the same thing. If he chose Peter to be the rock on which his Church was to be founded, thereby in effect nominating him to be the first of a long line of his Vicars on earth, there have been many mundane intruders into this spiritual domain, from the Emperor Constantine onwards. Now another takeover would seem to be imminent; by Caliban, this time, with, in place of Trinculo, Stephano, and their ribald crew, many a randy Father, mini-skirted nun and Marxist-dialoguing Jesuit in beret and parachutist rig. To those who like myself, rightly or wrongly, have become convinced that what is called 'Western civilization' is irretrievably over, and that another Dark Age is upon us, this seeming collapse of the Church is desolating. We bemoan the passing of a liturgy in which we never participated, of high virtues which we never practised, of an obedience we never accorded and an orthodoxy we never accepted and often ridiculed.

Yet even if it is true that, despite the assurance given to Peter, the gates of Hell have prevailed, or at any rate are now swinging on ecumenical hinges, that is only a lost battle. The war goes on; and suddenly, in the most unlikely theatre of all, a Solzhenitsyn raises his voice, while in the dismal slums of Calcutta a Mother Teresa and her Missionaries of Charity go about Jesus's work of love with incomparable dedication. When I think of them, as I have seen them at their work and at their devotions, I want to put away all the books, tear up all the scribbled notes. There are no more doubts or dilemmas; everything is perfectly clear. What commentary or exposition, however eloquent, lucid, perceptive, inspired even, can equal in eludication and illumination the effect of these dedicated lives? What mind has conceived a discourse, or tongue spoken it, which conveys even to a minute degree the light they shine before men? *I was an hungred, and ye gave me meat; I was thirsty, and ye gave me drink: I was a stranger, and ye took me in: naked and ye clothed me: I was sick, and ye visited me: I was in prison, and ye came unto me* – the words come alive, as no study or meditation could possibly make them, in the fulfilment in the most literal sense of Jesus's behest to see in the suffering face of humanity his suffering face, and in their broken bodies, his. The religion Jesus gave the world is an experience, not a body of ideas or principles. It is in being lived that it lives, as it is in loving that the love which it discloses at the heart of all creation becomes manifest. It belongs to the world of a Cervantes rather than that of a Wittgenstein; to Rabelais and Tolstoy rather than to Bultmann and Barth. It is for fools like Poor Tom rather than for his *Doppelgänger*, the Earl of Kent.

Thinking of Jesus, I suddenly understand that I know nothing, and for some reason begin to laugh hilariously, which brings me to the

realization that I understand everything I need to understand. So, in the face of a Mother Teresa I trace the very geography of Jesus's Kingdom; all the contours and valleys and waterways. I need no other map. In the light of such a faith as hers, the troubles of the Church, its liturgical squabbles and contending theologies and Vatican Councils drowsing through interminable sessions, seem of little account. Once when I was complaining about Church dignitaries and their attitudes, Mother Teresa drily pointed out that, of the twelve disciples, hand-picked by Jesus himself, one turned out to be a crook and the rest ran away. How, she asked, can we expect mere popes and bishops to do better? How indeed?

Jesus particularly charged his disciples that *they should tell no man he was . . . the Christ.* He, knew, of course, that if his Messianic role were to be bruited abroad the danger would arise of his becoming the focus of some sort of insurrection, which would falsify the whole purpose of his ministry. Being an attractive, forceful and persuasive speaker and teacher, with a strong personality, once he was seen as the Messiah, and known to have accepted that title, the violence anticipated in many of the Messianic prophecies might easily erupt about his head. To abate any possible ardour in this direction among the disciples, he broke it to them that he would shortly go to Jerusalem, and that there he would *suffer many things of the elders and chief priests and scribes, and be killed, and be raised again the third day.* Peter was outraged, and protested strongly; if Jesus was indeed the Messiah, as now they all accepted, they looked for him to be victorious, not defeated, and expected to share in his triumph. They were Sancho Panzas looking to receive their islands. *Be it far from thee Lord; this shall not be done unto thee,* Peter insisted; but this time Jesus rebuked him: *Get thee behind me, Satan: thou art an offence unto me: for thou savourest not the things that be of God, but those that be of men!* It effectively shut him up.

The danger that Jesus, once generally accepted as the Messiah, would be pushed into at any rate seeming to lead a rebellion, was a very real one. According to the Fourth Gospel, after the miracle of the loaves and fishes the excitement of the crowd was so great, and their conviction so strong that Jesus was indeed the prophet whose imminent coming into the world had been prophesied and was now eagerly awaited, that Jesus feared he might be taken by force and proclaimed a king. To avoid anything of the kind, *he departed again into a mountain, himself alone.* 'It is the simple historical fact', Professor William Barclay writes, 'that in the thirty years from 67 to 37 BC before the emergence of Herod the Great, no fewer than one hundred

73

and fifty thousand men perished in Palestine in revolutionary uprisings. There was no more explosive and inflammable country in the world than Palestine. If Jesus had publicly claimed to be Messiah, nothing could have stopped a useless flood tide of slaughter.' He goes on to point out that before he could openly claim the Messiahship, he had to show it to the world in a quite new light, with a quite new significance; as a Messiahship whose only power was sacrificial love. In other words, he was indubitably the Messiah, but one 'whose reign was in the hearts of men, a Messiah who reigned from a Cross'. Professor Barclay, along with the late Dr C. H. Dodd, provides the unfamiliar traveller across the deserts and jungles of Biblical criticism with one of his few sure, steady and infinitely reassuring beacons to guide him on his way.

Peter is the only one of the disciples whose character emerges clearly and strongly; the others are somewhat dim figures who in the Gospel narratives do and say little that distinguishes them from one another. This is the case even with John, the disciple Jesus is said to have loved with a special tenderness, and to whom he handed over the care of his mother as he was dying. Peter, on the other hand, is quite definitely a person – impetuous, mercurial, easily stirred to passionate protestations of devotion and loyalty, and equally prone to lose heart in face of difficulties, and to fall down on his undertakings when the test came. Just because of the clearer delineation of his character, he is always the easiest to pick out in group paintings of the disciples; for instance, in Leonardo da Vinci's *Last Supper*. At the same time, he is sympathetically portrayed, and there is, indeed, something irresistible about him even when he is at his worst; as in his tragic threefold denial of Jesus while Jesus was being examined by Caiaphas, the High Priest, and his father-in-law, Annas – a sinister figure who had managed, in a manner any contemporary political boss like Mayor Daley of Chicago might envy, after he had been High Priest himself for a number of years, to get the job for five of his sons in succession, as well as for his son-in-law Caiaphas. Peter stayed in the ante-room, and was warming his hands by a coal fire there when the first question was put to him by a maidservant guarding the door: *Art thou also one of this man's disciples?* His curt answer was *I am not.*

How vivid the scene is! – the flames of the lately lit fire illumining the faces of those silently gathered round it; within, the farcical interrogation going on, with occasional words heard, and the sound of Jesus being struck by one of the officers with the palm of his hand. All present must have been conscious that something momentous was happening. Then came the second question, from one of the people

74

A certain maid beheld him as he sat by the fire, and earnestly looked upon him, and said, This man was also with him. And he denied him, saying, Woman, I know him not.

PAINTING BY GEORGES
DE LA TOUR

gathered with Peter round the fire: *Art not thou also one of his disciples?* Again the denial, this time accompanied with shouts and curses; the resort of all of us when we succumb to cowardice and panic. Now the third and last question, from one of the High Priest's servants who had noticed Peter's Galilean accent, and thought he recognized him as having been in the Garden of Gethsemane with Jesus when he was taken: *Art not thou also one of his disciples?* No, he was not, Peter insisted, more vehemently than ever, pouring out a strong stream of abuse, curses and obscenities. Fishermen, like bargees, always know how to curse. At this point the dawn broke and the cock crowed, and Peter remembered how the evening before Jesus had prophesied that before the cock crowed he would have denied him thrice. So he went away and wept bitterly.

75

For Peter there was unforeseen comfort to come. After the Resurrection Jesus three times asked him if he loved him, thus balancing the three times Peter had denied him; and a chastened Peter each time answered less confidently than had been his way, saying that Jesus, who knew all things, must know that he loved him. To intimate his forgiveness of Peter and renewed faith in him, Jesus entrusted him with one of his most deeply felt commands: *Feed my sheep!* This, too, Jesus repeated three times to emphasize its urgency.

Another incident described in the Gospels, which Jesus particularly asked the three disciples who were present at it not to mention to anyone, at least until after his death and Resurrection, was what is called 'the Transfiguration'. The three disciples were Peter, James and John, and the incident occurred some eight days after the conversation at Caesarea Philippi. They had accompanied Jesus up into a high mountain; like all mystics, he needed from time to time to withdraw from the world, as he had into the wilderness after his baptism by John the Baptist. A high mountain, especially at dawn, offers a greater sense of isolation than even the desert or the high seas, and so is a favourite place for such withdrawals. On this occasion Jesus became so rapt that he was momentarily carried away into heavenly regions where he might commune more closely with God. Hearing him speaking as though with some unseen presence, and seeing his face shining with ecstasy, and even his clothes glistening and luminous, the three disciples were overcome with awe, so that they fell on their faces and were afraid. They had the impression that Jesus was conversing with Moses and Elijah, and Peter made the endearingly ludicrous suggestion that, in order to protract so remarkable a situation, he might construct three tabernacles for Jesus and the two prophets. At this point, we are told, a bright cloud overshadowed them all, and they seemed to hear a voice out of the cloud, like the one at Jesus's baptism, acknowledging him as God's beloved Son in whom He was well pleased, but on this occasion adding: *Hear ye him!* It was, after all, the essential requirement – to hear and heed what he had to say. It is so still.

Such transports as the Transfiguration are common enough among mystics, and there are numerous detailed descriptions of them, all of which bear a close resemblance to one another. This strongly suggests that the experience itself is related to some permanent, continuing element in human life which in a mystical state is clearly perceived, but only vaguely and occasionally glimpsed amidst the ordinary preoccupations of earthly living. As the existence of hunger

He was transfigured before them: and his face did shine as the sun, and his raiment was white as the light. And, behold, there appeared unto them Moses and Elias talking with him.

ILLUMINATION, C. 1000

presupposes the existence of bread, and the existence of a fiddle that of music, so the longing for God and awareness of God which characterizes all these mystical experiences presupposes His existence. How precious such experiences are! How one longs for their recurrence! And how mysteriously they come and go! Suddenly, everything seems clearly related to everything else; the harmony perfect, then as suddenly lost. The joy in the consciousness of this harmony is the greatest ever vouchsafed to us in this world, as the sense of loss when it passes is the greatest desolation.

At the Transfiguration, when the glory was upon Jesus, the luminosity was too much for the three disciples with him, and they had to shut their eyes. Still, they had seen and heard, and to that extent participated. Coming down from the mountain when it was all over, the reaction will have set in. I imagine them then, their footsteps laggardly, and their talk listless, looking closely at Jesus's familiar face and movements, and wondering whether it had really happened – that light, those voices, the words spoken from on high. Experiencing these brief ecstasies, so long watched and waited for, and passing so quickly, is like sitting through a dull concert because at some point there will be a movement, or maybe just a few chords, so sublime that the roof and the walls of the concert-hall will dissolve, the orchestra and their instruments and the prancing conductor with his baton disappear, leaving one alone in a universe overflowing with the music of life itself, its generality and its particularity merged into a oneness, eternal breakers beating against the shores of Time. Then back to the concert-hall, the violins and the cellos, the drums and the trumpets and the whistling flutes; mortality's familiar orchestration. Stretching a 'crumme of dust from heav'n to hell':

> Yet take thy way; for sure thy way is best:
> Stretch or contract me, thy poore debtor:
> This is but tuning of my breast,
> To make the music better.

So George Herbert saw it.

In Augustine's *Confessions* the experience is wonderfully described. It happened when he was at Ostia with his mother, Monica, after his conversion. They were on their way back to Africa; she triumphant, and soon to die, he full of peace and joy, with his long life's work before him. As they leaned from a window overlooking the courtyard of the house in which they were staying, their conversation turned on what the eternal life of the saints would be like, 'that life which no eye has seen, no ear has heard, no human heart conceived', and they concluded that no bodily pleasure, however delectable and lustrous

78

in earthly terms, was worthy of comparison, or even mention, beside the happiness of the life of the saints. As they talked on, their thoughts reached higher and higher; from 'the whole compass of material things in their various degrees, up to the heavens themselves, from which the sun and the moon and the stars shine down upon the earth'. Then higher still, full of the wonder of all creation, until they reached their own souls; pressing on even beyond them, towards the eternal Wisdom which belongs neither to the past nor the future, but simply *is*:

> And while we spoke of the eternal Wisdom, longing for it and straining for it with all the strength of our hearts, for one fleeting instant we reached out and touched it. Then with a sigh, leaving our spiritual harvest bound to it, we returned to the sound of our own speech, in which each word has a beginning and an ending – far, far different from your Word, our Lord, who abides in himself for ever, yet never grows old and gives new life to all things.

The descent to words – those clumsy and inflexible bricks – is like trying to play the *Missa Solemnis* on a mouth-organ, or to dance the *Mazurka* with no legs. A lifetime at the task but serves to make it seem the more impossible; truth in words at best attaining only meaning, beauty only elegance, and strength no more than shock. A daddy-long-legs struggling to climb out of a bath, or a mole diligently throwing up his heap of useless earth – so the artificer of words. Every spiritual harvest has, like Augustine's and Monica's, to be left behind, ungarnered; there is always the desolating return to the sound of words which begin and end when what they have to say has neither ending nor beginning. Happy the dumb who cannot be mocked by what they say; the illiterates who cannot be cheated by what they read, or cheat others with what they write!

Jesus spoke, but he also healed. The two went together; they were the equipoise between loving God and loving one's neighbour – the two duties into which Jesus resolved all that the Law laid down and the prophets had proclaimed. Even in the Garden of Gethsemane he healed, restoring the man's ear that Peter had impulsively hacked off with his sword. For that matter, even on the Cross he offered healing words to the penitent thief crucified beside him, making a rendezvous with him in paradise. Jesus never for one moment forgot our human need for bodies and minds in working order; for eyes that truly see and ears that truly hear. His compassion for the maimed, whether they were physically, mentally or spiritually disabled, was fathomless. More often than not, it was his healing powers which drew crowds to him. When it was known that he would be in a particular place they poured in from every direction, sometimes coming long distances – the blind groping their way, the halt and the lame and the infirm stumbling along as best they might, some carried on stretchers and litters; then the lepers, shunned by the others, with stumps for arms and lost noses and hobbling toeless feet. Such macabre gatherings assemble at festivals in India, chattering and pleading in the expectation of alms or miracles or both. At Lourdes, too, bowing their heads, abating their twitchings, holding out their hands, if they have any, as the Blessed Sacrament approaches.

The sick who crowded round Jesus wanted, of course, to get near him, if possible to touch or be touched; in any case to catch his particular attention. There was, for instance, the woman with a long-standing issue of blood who managed to get close behind him and reached out her hand to his clothing, calculating: *If I may touch his clothes, I shall be whole.* It worked; *straightway the fountain of her blood was dried up; and she felt in her body that she was healed.* Jesus at once knew something had happened; he was conscious of power going out of him, and asked who had touched his garments. In view of the crush of people, the disciples considered this rather a ridiculous question, but the woman herself, *fearing and trembling, knowing what was done in her, came and fell down before him, and told him all the truth.* Whereupon Jesus told her: *Daughter, thy faith hath made thee whole; go in peace, and be whole of thy plague,* which I am sure she did, never forgetting till the end of her days the deliverance that had come to her; possibly boring people by talking constantly about it. Not that issue of blood again! *Reductio ad absurdum* is built by God into our lives and all our history.

The first requirement in Jesus's miraculous cures – underlined in the particular case of the woman with an issue of blood precisely because she had no other contact with him than just to touch his clothing – was faith on the part of the recipient that Jesus could effect a cure. Any doubt on this point ruled out all possibility of one. Good doctors always say that they don't and can't cure their patients, but only provide the circumstances for them to cure themselves. It is the same with miracles; an age that believes in miracles is likely to witness them, and an age like ours which dismisses the possibility, correspondingly unlikely. We get, not only the government, but the miracles we deserve. Although the woman with an issue of blood made no appeal to Jesus, established no contact with him, yet just touching his clothing sufficed to cure her. Jesus, for his part, was at once conscious that thereby something had been taken from him. In other words, just as the person cured had to believe in the possibility of a cure, so

Daughter, thy faith hath made thee whole; go in peace, and be whole of thy plague.

STONE CARVING,
HILDESHEIM CATHEDRAL

80

the curer, in effecting one, had to give of himself, of his love, of his vitality; as it might be, of his heart's blood. Walking with Mother Teresa among her lepers, it was obvious to me that her mere presence soothed and revived them. Just by being with them she gave them life and hope. Afterwards I could see that she was drained of life herself. She never admits that she is tired, or that what she has to give can be used up; but at times a greyness comes into her face, and her eyes momentarily go out like a lamp when there is no more oil. Is it surprising that, confronted with the task of reviving Lazarus, Jesus groaned aloud at the prospect of so spending himself?

In the early days of blood-transfusion, before the use of plasma, the donor was connected visibly to the recipient by a glass tube. Then the doctor would pump, so that the donor actually saw the blood being drawn out and pumped into another body, producing almost instantaneous revival; colour and expression and shape coming back into a grey, lost face. If the face was familiar – often pored over; creased and crumpled, like a much-used map – then the experience was ecstatic, almost sensual in its intensity. Once, in this situation, I heard myself shouting out to the pathologist operating the transfusion to keep at it, and draw blood lavishly without any concern about the available supply. If, however, it was the face of a stranger – in the particular case I am thinking of, a man in his middle fifties, with a sparse red beard growing spikily out of wan cheeks and chin – curiously enough the experience was in some ways more harrowing. There was something infinitely moving and tender in thus disgorging blood for a nebulous figure, never seen before, never to be seen again. Just a man, any man, ashen-lipped, with glazed eyes and bad breath. Someone who would pass for being totally insignificant, of a kind encountered in railway compartments, whose remarks, if he made any, were bound to be banal, but for whom none the less I was giving my blood, and in the process feeling for him an overwhelming concern and love. If I had known him at all, or wanted to know him, detected in him some particular charm or grace, seen some specific reason why the protraction of his life was desirable – he would write books, make discoveries, he had children to support and work to finish – our tubular connection and blood-sharing would have been less uplifting. The Unknown Soldier interred in Westminster Abbey or under the Arc de Triomphe; the Unknown Recipient to whom blood is dispensed, in hospitals and at altar rails.

Jesus's healing may be compared, though of course on an immeasurably higher spiritual level, with this giving of blood to a stranger. With certain particular exceptions like the raising of

82

Lazarus, the people he healed were unknown to him. It might be two blind men shouting after him to have their sight restored, or a fellow worshipper in a synagogue who happened to have a withered arm, or some poor, possessed soul yelling and grinding his teeth, or an infirm man who had come year after year to a sheep-market pool in Jerusalem where it was said an angel from time to time troubled the waters, and that whoever bathed in them first after the troubling would be healed of whatever disease he might have – but this poor man had no one to help him down to the pool, so that year after year he missed his chance. These were cases which for one reason or another attracted Jesus's attention, so that the two blind men got back their sight, the withered arm was held out and healed even though it was the Sabbath, the poor possessed soul became sane, and the infirm man by the pool was instructed to rise, take up his bed and walk, which he duly did, also on the Sabbath. On other occasions when the sick gathered, we are simply told in the Gospels that he healed them, without specifying how many or what their ailments were.

Sometimes Jesus's healing involved touching the afflicted parts, or some simple action like using his spittle to make mud which he put on a blind man's sightless eyes to bring back their sight. There was, of course, no question of treatment in the medical sense, still less of drugs or medicine. His commonest, indeed, his almost invariable, procedure was to tell those who were to be cured that their sins were forgiven them; by thus relieving them of their moral infirmities they were automatically relieved of their physical ones. This was especially infuriating to the legalistic Scribes; they considered it amounted to blasphemously making himself equal with God, who alone was competent to forgive sins. Jesus brushed their objections aside with: *For whether is easier, to say, Thy sins be forgiven thee; or to say, Arise, and walk?* In any case the man in question, who was sick of the palsy and lying in a bed, did arise and walk, thereby proving Jesus's point. Jesus likewise brushed aside the legalistic objection of the Scribes to healing on the Sabbath. Would they not, any one of them, go after one of their cattle that had fallen into a ditch on the Sabbath? Of course they would! How much more, then, was it permissible on the Sabbath, as on any other day, to save a fellow human being who had fallen into sickness or demon-possession.

Such acts of healing on Jesus's part are generally considered to be miracles, which of course they are in the sense that they happened at his behest, and that in the account given of them in the Gospels they are seen as coming about through the direct intervention of God, and so as transcending what is called the natural law. On this showing,

although my resuscitation of the red-bearded man with bad breath by giving him my blood happened more or less instantaneously, it was not a miracle, but came into the category of normal medical treatment. If it is considered that in effecting his miracles Jesus was bound, consciously or unconsciously, to give of himself – for instance, on the occasion described in St Luke's Gospel, when *a great multitude of people out of all Judaea and Jerusalem, and from the sea coast of Tyre and Sidon . . . came to hear him, and to be healed of their diseases. . . . And all the multitude sought to touch him, for there went virtue out of him, and healed them all* – then the two processes of a blood-transfusion and a miracle can be seen as comparable. Indeed, had Jesus been a

Then touched he their eyes, saying, According to your faith be it unto you. And their eyes were opened.

MOSAIC, ST APOLLINARE NUOVO, RAVENNA

84

Harley Street specialist instead of an itinerant evangelist claiming to
be the Son of God, he might well have carried on his healing in
precisely the same way, getting himself knighted instead of founding
a world religion, a church and a civilization. In both cases, he would
equally have fallen foul of the authorities; the British Medical
Association, we may be sure, would have found his methods and
pretensions as abhorrent as the Sanhedrin did, and would likewise
have sought ways to dispose of him.

If Jesus's miracles may thus be seen as a sort of spiritual equivalent
of a blood-transfusion, in his case it was not just a matter of dispensing
a pint or so of surplus blood, and then having a cheerful cup of tea with

85

Matron. Ultimately, on the Cross, he gave all his blood, to the very last drop, not to revive one patient for the remainder of a waning life, but to revivify all mankind for ever; the outward and visible sign of this being the Eucharist, when Jesus's blood in the form of the Blessed Sacrament is offered to all who will accept it.

Through the miracles we may understand the availability of forgiveness, the possibility of redemption and the promise of salvation. They are, in this sense, a kind of parable, conveying, as the others do, how we may be whole persons rather than maimed and disjointed, floundering and staggering like a bird with a broken wing. In the spoken parables he told us how to achieve this – how to see clearly through the eye rather than blindly with it, how to live fleet and free as children of God rather than burdened and manacled as bond slaves to our will and desires. The miracles were practical demonstrations to the same effect; here, a blind man who sees, a dumb man who speaks, a crazed man who puts on his clothes and recovers his right mind, here a lame man who runs, a dead man who lives again. *Come unto me, all ye that labour and are heavy laden, and I will give you rest. Take my yoke upon you, and learn of me; for I am meek and lowly in heart; and ye shall find rest unto your souls* – who can resist such an invitation, so wonderfully conveyed in word and deed?

It was Jesus's mercy thus to use miracles or parables rather than propounding ideas or deploying arguments, which he only indulged in ironically or humorously in exchanges with legalistic Scribes who were trying to trip him up. The only history he drew on, or for that matter knew, was the traditional story of the Children of Israel as set forth in the Hebrew Scriptures. Not one date or generalization; no anthropology, sociology, psychology; just the world and its ways, as he and his hearers knew them. A grain of wheat was put in the earth and died, in its death germinating; so we died, and in dying, lived. Rain fell on the just and unjust alike; so did God's love. A shepherd would leave his flock to go after one lost sheep, find it and bring it back to the fold; so God concerned Himself with one sinner, which we all are – solitary sinners who easily stray and lose our way. The lilies of the field neither toil nor spin, but yet are arrayed more gloriously than Solomon; so God who has clothed plants in such magnificence will surely clothe us, His children.

The scientific view of life as a closed system governed by an inexorable natural law tends to rule out belief in miracles, which most people nowadays regard as the inventions of too credulous early Christians and too ardent later ones. Even believers search eagerly for some scientifically tenable explanation of the miraculous occurrences which played so large a part in Jesus's ministry. Yet, as St Augustine pointed out, when Jesus turned water into wine at the wedding feast in Cana of Galilee he was only performing quickly the slow miracle occurring year by year in vineyards, whereby the irrigation water fills out the grapes for the sun to ripen them, so that they may be transformed into wine. The same thing might be said about the miraculous cures. Psychiatrists require many sessions to relieve a patient of guilt feelings which have made him sick in body and mind; Jesus's power of spiritual and moral persuasion was so overwhelming that he could produce the same effect just by saying: *Thy sins be forgiven thee*. Likewise, far more effectively and lastingly than any sedative, he could calm and soothe the mentally distracted by ordering the demons who were tormenting them to be gone.

Mental sickness of one sort and another is the particular scourge of our time; as the tuberculosis sanatoria empty, the psychiatric wards fill with frustrated pursuers of happiness. There must be few today who have not had some personal experience of such institutions, and so are familiar with the particular anguish of seeing a beloved face drugged into vacancy or twisted and contorted with some uncomprehended and incomprehensible fury. In the light of their distress, the notion of demonic possession, generally held throughout the Roman Empire when Jesus was preaching and teaching and healing in Galilee and Judaea, will not seem so wide of the mark as might be supposed by comparison with our allegedly more profound understanding of the cause and cure of mental disorders. Who, helpless before another's mental affliction, would not welcome the coming of someone like Jesus, capable by his mere presence of calming a distracted mind; driving away the ravenous, angry impulses which are its torment, and bringing back to a face darkened with animality the light of recognition and the capacity to respond to love? Then ask, and he will come; that was the promise.

Jesus seems to have been especially compassionate towards the mentally sick; and when he sent the disciples off to preach on his behalf, he specifically empowered them to cast out demons from any who were troubled by them. He clearly felt a particular sympathy for these unfortunates, often homeless like himself, and left to wander in desolate places. For instance, the one he encountered in the country of the Gadarenes who went about naked, frequented the cemetery, and was subject to fits so violent that he easily broke any bonds or chains used to restrain him. A wild figure indeed, who when he saw Jesus shouted out: *What have I to do with thee, Jesus, thou Son of the most high God?* An ordinary person would have been

All the devils besought him, saying, Send us into the swine, that we may enter into them. And forthwith Jesus gave them leave.

IVORY CARVING

afraid and have made off — I certainly should — but Jesus stayed and asked the man his name. He said it was 'Legion' on account of being possessed, not just by one demon, but by many — which I take to be some sort of joke of a kind that the deranged greatly enjoy, laughing uproariously and cracking their fingers to intimate their satisfaction. At this point, according to the account in the Gospels, the demons themselves joined in the conversation, beseeching Jesus not to order them into the nearby Lake of Galilee, but rather into a herd of swine feeding on the mountainside. He agreed to this, and the demons were duly transferred to the swine, who thereupon ran violently down a steep path into the water and were drowned. So they found themselves in the lake anyway, providing for all time an image of the self-destructiveness of the human will.

When the local inhabitants saw the man whom they regarded as a dangerous homicidal maniac beyond all hope of recovery, now, after his encounter with Jesus, *clothed, and in his right mind*, and heard of what had happened to the herd of swine, *then the whole multitude of the country of the Gadarenes round about besought him to depart from them; for they were taken with great fear.* Jesus duly departed by boat, back across the Lake, doubtless reflecting that it was not only in his own country that a prophet was without honour, but also wherever he had allowed his insights and healing powers to become apparent; in this case by pacifying and making sane someone who had become a byword for the fury and ferocity of his ways. The man himself, understandably enough, wanted to stay with Jesus to whom he owed so much, but this was forbidden, and he was told to return to his own house and show by his continuing sanity what great things God had done for him.

Jesus saw sickness as an outward and visible sign of the imperfection which belongs to our human condition. He came to show us perfection, to be attained, not by perfecting our bodily existence (assuming that to be possible, as some overweening contemporary minds have supposed), which in practice would only serve to remove us further away than ever from perfection as Jesus understood it; achieving a kind of grainy Scandinavian excellence, a matt or glossy Playmate finish attained by using this or that hair-wash or skin-food, visiting this or that resort, and otherwise falling in with the persuasion of the advertisers and the Media pundits of progress. Rather, reaching after perfection by dying in order to be reborn, sloughing off the old man, our fleshly being, as a snake does its old skin irrespective of whether it is frail or robust, ungainly or comely, drab or dazzling. In giving the blind back their sight Jesus made us understand that we are

89

all anyway in need of seeing eyes. When the crippled and even the dead rose up at his behest, they illustrated a truth more ineffable than any miracle – that in suffering and dying we live, while in living and abounding for life's own sake alone we sicken and die.

This truth is evident most dramatically among the mentally sick, which is doubtless why Jesus was especially compassionate towards them. Their blank faces and stumbling words, their clumsy gestures and movements, their very fury and violence, have a weird kind of inner beauty, and even grace, as their wild laughter and grotesqueries – exaggerated courtesies and formalities, like kissing hands very elaborately, bowing and scraping and uncovering, can seem, in a poignant sort of way, truly funny. Among Moslems lunatics are positively revered, as in pre-psychiatric times English village idiots were affectionately regarded. In the sane, different impulses are blended; the loving smile can turn into a scowl, the sweet affection into clamant lechery, without its being clear where one begins and the other ends. In the deranged, on the other hand, everything is separate and demarcated; the body and the soul, the will and the imagination, desire and love, disengaged. Their consequent schizophrenia is a kind of confused integrity, which makes social life difficult, if not impossible for them. Hence the urge to accommodate them in special institutions, where, with a kind of moral gentility, they are designated 'mentally handicapped' rather than mad.

Jesus was spared becoming acquainted with such institutions for the insane, who in his time, like the man in the country of the Gadarenes, ran wild – an arrangement doubtless inconvenient for others, and perhaps cruel to them, though in other respects preferable to herding them together, to be confined, drugged and subjected to treatment of various kinds according to whatever happens to be in vogue at the moment. Even then, puzzled and lethargic, they have their strange beauty, which comes of being uninvolved and uncommitted. They are earthy mystics whose Cloud of Unknowing is a ground-mist rather than aerial; often frowning, their features set in some sort of vague, clumsy longing, as though they were pining, like animals in the zoo. But for what? Maybe for freedom, maybe for dinner, maybe for love, maybe just for oblivion. Who can tell? In any case, pining.

I have a particularly vivid memory of worshipping with them one Sunday morning in Bethel, near Bielefeld in Germany, where there is a large Lutheran settlement for mental cases of all kinds. The service was held under the trees, where an altar, a pulpit and seats are arranged for outdoor worship when weather permits. Most of the congregation were inmates, the epileptics wearing leather headgear like footballers in case they fell while the service was in progress. An inmates' band accompanied the singing, which was spirited but erratic; through the sermon and the prayers there were occasional broken shouts, and much twitching and turning. Yet I had a sense of great devotion; it was all very beautiful and uplifting. Walking away afterwards, I saw two white-haired deaconesses seated on a bench with some of the inmates considered to be unfit to attend the service. Under the direction of the deaconesses they were all joyously singing together, reminding me of Bunyan's description in *Grace Abounding* of how before he was converted he heard some women singing on a Sunday morning in Bedford. I dare say the notes were somewhat cracked, but I think I never heard such beautiful singing, and wondered whether any more acceptable songs of praise rose to heaven that Sunday morning. It was a place, I decided, where Jesus would have been very much at home. Indeed, I think I can say that he *was* at home there. Similarly, at L'Arche – the Ark – the community in the Forest of Compiègne founded by Jean Vanier, where the ostensibly sane and the ostensibly insane live, work and worship together in the spirit of Jesus, the Masses in their little chapel are unforgettably beautiful in their joyousness, devotion and Christian unity.

There is the further question whether Jesus himself may not have been in some sense mad. This is not an irreverence. Many of the noblest and most inspired people, like Blake and Dr Johnson, St Francis and the Apostle Paul, have been considered mad. The only recorded comment by de Gaulle on Simone Weil, the most luminous intelligence of our time, who served for a while in the Second World War with the Gaullists in London, was: *'Elle est folle!'* William Cowper was put in a strait-jacket, the coming on of his periods of insanity being signalized by the production of some of his most beautiful hymns – like 'God moves in a mysterious way'. Nietzsche died in a mad-house and in our own time Ezra Pound was put in one for refusing to unsay what he had said in his broadcasts from Rome during the Second World War. The Soviet Government likewise has availed itself of psychiatric institutions to get rid of its choicest spirits.

Sanity is Eternity's surrender to time, and I cannot believe that a man who was God would strike other men as wholly sane. The saintliest soldier I ever knew, when he was serving in Kenya, was diagnosed as a head case, as an alternative to being put on a charge – actually, for distributing to some hungry Africans lurking round the cookhouse door the contents of swill-buckets intended for the pigs.

Again, at the first Pentecost, when the disciples met together, and *there came a sound from heaven as of a rushing mighty wind. . . . And there appeared unto them cloven tongues, like as of fire, and it sat upon each of them,* and they all began to speak *as the Spirit gave them utterance,* sceptical observers considered they must be, if not mad, then *full of new wine.* Peter indignantly repudiated the suggestion, pointing out that anyway they could not possibly be drunk *seeing it is but the third hour of the day* – an alibi familiar to all old topers.

Jesus's apocalyptic utterances will have seemed very wild to his contemporaries – for instance, his account of the last days which, he insisted, were to occur within the lifetime of some who were then living, when *the sun shall be darkened, and the moon shall not give her light, and the stars of heaven shall fall and the powers that are in heaven shall be shaken.* This was to be the prelude to his own return to earth, *coming in the clouds with great power and glory,* and seated on a throne of judgment. There were also to be twelve thrones on which the twelve disciples would judge the twelve tribes of Israel. Such visions of a final dramatic *dénouement* in the story of mankind were common enough in Jesus's time, and are by no means unknown today. In Jesus's case there was the confusing factor that in other moods he might deprecate these lurid prophecies, or ask his disciples to keep them to themselves, as he asked them to keep to themselves his claims to be the Messiah and on intimate terms with God as His only begotten Son. At times he would identify himself with the lowliest among men; at other times proclaim himself a greater preacher than Jonah, and wiser than Solomon. On occasion he would boast of his miraculous cures, and then particularly ask the person cured under no circumstances to advertise what had happened. All this is human enough; we are all given both to boasting and to self-depreciation, and sometimes to indulging in the one in the guise of the other – which is worse than either. In his Manhood, Jesus was liable to such infirmities, as in his Godhood he was capable of realizing a total disinterestedness which took him into sublime regions of the spirit beyond the reach of any mere man. The writers of the Gospels, too, in their love and admiration for Jesus, will have wanted to endow him with every kind of greatness, however contradictory; to make him, at one and the same time, the mightiest and the lowliest of men, very God and very Man. Adulation, even at its most exalted, is undiscriminating.

I have myself encountered a number of crazy people who claimed to be someone else; as de Gaulle, or Napoleon, or Alexander the Great. Blake likewise would disconcert his visitors by casually remarking when they visited him that he had some historical celebrity with him, like Edward the Confessor or Robert Bruce, whose portrait he was engaged in painting. Once I was visited by someone who told me, in the greatest confidence, that he was Jesus Christ, and that it had been revealed to him that I was the Apostle Paul, my acceptance of this role being my reward for acknowledging my visitor as being indeed Jesus. To get rid of such awkward intruders I easily decided they were mad. Subsequently I had qualms of conscience, thinking: Suppose it was Jesus! And I sent him away! After all, this was just how Jesus would have appeared during his ministry to unbelievers – as a megalomaniac crackpot prattling of being God's Son, and authorized to speak on His behalf. Alas, had I lived in the time of Jesus, I fear I should have been among the scoffers, and missed the glory of those who heard and saw him and believed.

As for Jesus's apocalyptic utterances – all imaginative minds are prone to them, as, equally, to utopian fantasies. A heightened consciousness of human imperfection points to the imminence of some cosmic catastrophe, as a heightened awareness of human potentialities points to the possibility of living happily ever after. These two impulses may be seen at their most vulgar in someone like H. G. Wells, who, on the one hand, envisaged the coming to pass of a scientifically planned and directed kingdom of heaven on earth, and, on the other, in face of the achievement of atomic fission – in itself, no great matter – turned his face to the wall and insisted that mind was now at the end of its tether, and that the last days were upon us, with only the prospect of beginning the evolutionary process all over again in the hope that it might produce some creature more satisfactory and amenable than the shortly to become extinct *Homo sapiens*. The same impulses existed in Marx's over-heated mind. He likewise imagined the final emergence of a perfect human society when the proletariat of the world took their destined place as the definitive ruling class whose beneficent rule would go on for ever and ever. At the same time, in the light of the actual condition of the world in the later stages of the Industrial Revolution, he could only foresee conflicts and disasters. It would be ridiculous, as well as in the worst of taste, to equate Jesus with Wells and Marx, but it may properly be said that during his sojourn on earth, like them, he partook of the alternations of mood belonging to a discerning, intuitive and audacious mind.

At times the splendour of our human destiny presented itself to him as a prospect of eternal life, when our music would be the songs of angels, and what was imperfect in us would be made perfect, and we should neither hunger nor thirst, know neither fear nor hatred, neither marry nor be given in marriage, but attune ourselves to the harmony, the joy, the effulgence of God's universal love in His very presence. At other times, the blindness and obtuseness of men, even of his chosen Twelve, their inability to grasp what he meant or to comprehend even the simplest imagery of his parables, their proneness to lick the earth rather than reach up to the heavens, to fold their egos round them and lock themselves up in the dark prison of their own carnality, minding not the things of God but the things of men – all this led him to ask: *What shall it profit a man, if he shall gain the whole world, and lose his own soul? Or what shall a man give in exchange for his soul?* Lest anyone should think that these were remote contingencies, arising in a remote future, he went on to say that the Son of Man would be coming in the very near future *in the glory of his Father with his angels; and then he shall reward every man according to his works.* And to rub in the point that this was going to happen soon, he continued: *There be some standing here, which shall not taste of death, till they see the Son of man coming in his kingdom.*

It was a warning which struck home; the early Christians were, to their great edification, to be worried for half a century and more as to whether they would thus be called to account while still living in this world. To haunt them, there were those fateful words about knowing *neither the day nor the hour wherein the Son of man cometh,* and about how ill it would fare with any who might be found unprepared and forgetful when the moment arrived. Also, about how in that time there would be *wars and rumours of wars. . . . For nation shall rise against nation, and kingdom against kingdom; and there shall be famines, and pestilences, and earthquakes, in divers places* – a state of affairs so dangerous and unaccountable that if anyone were on the housetop it would be highly imprudent to come down and take anything out of the house, or if in the fields to turn back to collect some clothing. *And woe unto them that are with child, and to them that give suck in those days. But pray ye that your flight be not in the winter, neither on the Sabbath day: for then shall be great tribulation, such as was not since the beginning of the world to this time, no, nor ever shall be.*

If, for the early Christians, with Jesus's actual words of warning still echoing in their ears, the prospect of the coming apocalypse was very actual, in the subsequent centuries there have always been some unhinged or prophetic souls who felt certain that the last days would shortly be upon them. Today the feeling is particularly strong, not without reason. The truth is that famines and pestilences and wars and rumours of wars have been the constant lot of mankind. Crisis is not the exception, but our permanent condition; and awareness of this, as Dr Johnson said of waiting to be hanged, wonderfully concentrates the mind. To believe that men living in time can know lasting peace, prosperity and contentment is far more fallacious and demented than to expect the end of the world in the near future. The world is always about to end, but utopias never even begin; and so the Devil, who feels most at home in fantasy, and sees more mileage in the *Guardian* than in the *News of the World*, in Eleanor Roosevelt than in Marilyn Monroe, in the World Council of Churches than the Mafia, as being more amenable to his purposes, can work more readily through utopians than through apocalyptists, as the post-Rousseau era has all too clearly shown.

I cannot see how the Church could possibly have survived through all the decadence, disorder and wickedness of the last centuries of the Roman Empire if there had not been this built-in expectation of a Second Coming and the end of history. Otherwise, the early Christians, like the later ones, would have got themselves enmeshed in the risings and rebellions and illusory earthly expectations which are the invariable accompaniment of a decomposing civilization. Who, expecting the end of the world today or tomorrow, is going to concern himself about further nationalizing the means of production, freedom-fighting, raising the school age to nineteen and lowering the age of consent to ten, and other such enlightened enterprises? The only way to be sane about history is to keep its end in view, as the only way to be sane about living is to keep death in view. Jesus catered for this need by promising to return to us, and soon rather than late, so that we should be under the necessity of always expecting him, and constantly made aware that the span of life, like the span of the Bible, is from a Garden of Eden to an Apocalypse; its course from innocence, through knowledge of Good and Evil, to the Incarnation.

The fluctuations in Jesus's moods about his miracles are equally marked. Sometimes he boasted that if like wonders had been performed in Sodom as in Capernaum, then Sodom would have remained until this day, whereas Capernaum will go down into Hades; at other times he told those he had cured, at all costs to keep to themselves their miraculous deliverance, and resolutely refused to provide, through miracles or in any other way, a sign of his special relationship with God and the divine inspiration of his mission on earth. Indeed, the impression conveyed by the Gospels is that Jesus performed his miracles with a certain diffidence, and even reluctance. Compassion urged him on. There was suffering and pain and anguish which he could cure. So how could he withold his help? At the same time, he had to take account of the danger that his miracles would impress the crowds rather than what he had to say and what he had himself to be and endure before his ministry was fulfilled. By pronouncing forgiveness of sins he could make the blind see, the lame walk, the demented sane; yet, as he well knew, when this happened, the popular reaction was not to abjure the sins which had been forgiven, but rather to marvel at the cure that had been effected.

None the less, Jesus could not refrain; the blind crying for their sight, the cripples for their legs, the mad for their sanity, were more than he could endure. So, with a sigh, and sometimes a groan, he used his healing hands and voice, and his blessed gift of forgiveness. In this sense, it may be said that Jesus was most human when, in performing his miracles, he seemed to be resorting to the supernatural, and that his divinity showed most clearly in what will have appeared to his contemporaries as most ordinary – his day-by-day evangelism and giving out of love.

It might even be said that the supernatural altogether is only an indefinite extension of the natural, whereas it is in Jesus's words, as transmitted to us, perhaps imperfectly, perhaps with an eye to other purposes than he had in mind, and in his Passion which embodied these words in the great drama of the Crucifixion and the Resurrection, that we may detect in him qualities of more than earthly dimensions. That Jesus performed miracles is the least of reasons for believing him to be God. There have been many miracles, up to and including the so-called 'miracles of science' of our own time – like sending our words coursing through space faster than we can speak them, and coursing through space ourselves even faster – and doubtless in the future there will be others still more remarkable; but only of one man – Jesus – has it been said that he had the words of eternal life. These words would still stand, and ever must, if he had never healed a single sick person, or alternatively, healed as many as penicillin has.

Of all Jesus's reported miracles the most dramatic was undoubtedly the raising of Lazarus from the dead – only recounted in the Fourth Gospel. Lazarus lived with his two sisters, Mary and Martha, at Bethany, a village within walking distance of Jerusalem on the slopes of the Mount of Olives. It was a household where Jesus was particularly welcome, and where he stayed when he was in Jerusalem, partly because he loved the three of them and was happy in their company, and doubtless also because there was always some danger for him in Jerusalem, so that it was more congenial for him to sleep away from the city. The account in the Gospels of Jesus's relations with Mary and Martha is told with exceptional artistry, like a perfect little novel.

In character the two sisters are very different, as is brought out in an episode when Jesus was visiting them. Martha is the one who *received him into her house*, but Mary *sat at Jesus's feet and heard his word*, which somehow irritated Martha, busy preparing a meal – *cumbered about much serving*. One sees the scene exactly; one sister lost to the world entirely in her enthralment with Jesus's words; the other bustling about, getting red in the face, sleeves turned up, and I dare say in her irritation banging the dishes about noisily, until she can stand it no longer and blurts out: *Lord, dost thou not care that my sister hath left me to serve alone? Bid her therefore that she help me*. Jesus's response was somewhat enigmatic, and I doubt whether it served to restore Martha's equanimity: *Martha, Martha, thou art careful and troubled about many things; but one thing is needful, and Mary hath chosen that good part, which shall not be taken away from her*. It is reasonable to assume, I think, that though Jesus loved both sisters, he had a special affection for Mary, who possessed the gift, dear to all men, of creative listening; of absorbing ardently not just words and ideas, but the ultimate sense of what someone they care for says, as a tree absorbs the sunlight into its leaves.

Jesus had withdrawn to the district beyond Jordan where he had been baptized by John the Baptist, when the news was brought to him that Lazarus, the brother of Mary and Martha, was sick. Their message was: *Lord, behold, he whom thou lovest is sick*. Instead of, as might be expected, hurrying at once to Bethany, Jesus stayed on where he was for a couple of days. Then he announced to the disciples that they were going into Judaea again even though, as they all knew, it was dangerous, his enemies being now out to stone him. The disciples, indeed, protested that it was folly to take such a risk, but Jesus brushed their fears aside; his time had not yet come, and until it did no serious ill could befall him. He went on to tell them that *our friend Lazarus sleepeth; but I go, that I may awake him out of sleep*. As so often happened, the disciples did not get what he meant, and took it that Lazarus was literally sleeping, and so might be assumed to be better. Jesus thereupon told them bluntly that Lazarus was dead, and that he was glad for their sakes that he had not been with him at the time, since now the miracle of raising him up would strengthen their faith the more. The matter thus seemed settled, and Thomas, the disciple who was later to disbelieve in the risen Jesus until he had actually touched his wounds, fatalistically said to the others: *Let us also go, that we may die with him*. In the event, far from dying with him, they would scatter in panic, and poor Peter go through the misery of denying him thrice.

When they arrived at Bethany they found that Lazarus had been in his tomb for four days. It was Martha who came to meet Jesus; Mary stayed where she was in the house – another manifestation of the contrasting characters of the two sisters, one active and the other passive, one purposeful and the other contemplative. *Lord, if thou hadst been here, my brother had not died*, Martha said; *but I know that even now, whatsoever thou wilt ask of God, God will give it thee*. Jesus responded by assuring her that her brother would rise again. Mary would have understood perfectly what he meant; Martha took his words to be conventional consolation, and answered almost testily that of course she knew he would rise again in the Resurrection at the last day along with everyone else. It was then that Jesus delivered himself of the words which are the core of the whole episode, whose importance far transcends the actual events, whatever they may precisely have been. *I am the resurrection, and the life; he that believeth in me, though he were dead, yet shall he live; and whosoever liveth and believeth in me shall never die*. Words which at every Christian interment for twenty centuries have brought comfort and hope to the bereaved as they are spoken across open graves.

This answer of Jesus to death was an essential part of his ministry. Death had haunted the pagan world; as something to be dreaded, stoically faced, put out of mind, despairingly embraced; at best, in the manner of Socrates, greeted with noble resignation: 'The hour of departure has arrived, and we go our ways – I to die, and you to live. Which is the better, God only knows.' Jesus audaciously abolished death, transforming it from a door that slammed to, into one that opened to whoever knocked. He made death, as Bonhoeffer joyously said on his way to be executed, for a Christian a beginning, not an end. It was the key to life; to die was to live. This was what so impressed Tolstoy in the Christian concept of dying. Furthermore, Tolstoy observed that, whereas he and the tiny intellectual élite to which he belonged were horrified by the prospect of dying because they had seen no point in living, his peasants confronted death with equanimity, well content that their days should end, and serenely confident that their further existence, whatever shape it might have, would be part of God's loving purpose for them. His own despair at the prospect of the obliteration of his clamant ego was so overwhelming that he had to hide away a rope hanging in his study for fear of hanging himself with it. It was then that he turned back to the Gospels, and as Jesus spoke to him through their pages, the dark menacing figure of death was transformed into the shining promise of life, now in this world, and thereafter.

98

In our post-Christian era death has recovered its old terrors, becoming unmentionable, as sex has become ever more mentionable. Private parts are public, but death is the twentieth century's dirty little secret. What is more, the fantasy is sustained that as science has facilitated fornication without procreation, in due course it will facilitate life without death, and enable the process of extending our life span to go on and on for ever, so that it never does come to an end. Thus Dr Christiaan Barnard's heart-transplant operations, which caused so much excitement at the time, seemed to hold out the hope of replacing our parts as they wore out, and thus of keeping us on the road indefinitely, like old vintage cars. New hearts, kidneys, genitals, brain-boxes even, installed as and when required, the requisite spare-parts being taken from the newly dead, or maybe from mental defec-tives and other afflicted persons who might be said for one reason or another to be making no good use of them. The resultant immortal beings would have no occasion to be raised from the dead as Lazarus was. Nor would Jesus's wonderful words about being the resurrec-tion and the life have any significance. For them, there was no dying, and therefore no rising from the dead. Nor will those who dream of living without dying be attracted by, or even comprehend, the notion of dying in order to live.

For myself, as I approach my own end, which cannot now be long delayed, I find Jesus's outrageous claim to be, himself, the resurrec-tion and the life, ever more captivating and meaningful. Quite often, waking up in the night as the old do, and feeling myself to be half out of my body, so that it is a mere chance whether I go back into it to live through another day, or fully disengage and make off; hovering thus between life and death, seeing our dear earth with its scents and sounds and colours, as I have known and loved them, more, perhaps, as Bernanos said, than I have dared to admit; recalling the golden hours of human love and human work, at the same time vouchsafed a glimpse of what lies ahead, Eternity rising in the distance, a great expanse of ineffable light – so placed, Jesus's words ring triumphantly through the universe, spanning my two existences, the one in Time drawing to a close and the one in Eternity at its glorious beginning. So at last I may understand, and understanding, believe; see my ancient carcass, prone between the sheets, stained and worn like a scrap of paper dropped in the gutter, muddy and marred with being trodden underfoot, and, hovering over it, myself, like a butterfly released from its chrysalis stage and ready to fly away. Are caterpillars told of their impending resurrection? How in dying they will be transformed from poor earth-crawlers into creatures of the air, with exquisitely painted wings? If told, do they believe it? Is it conceivable to them that so constricted an existence as theirs should burgeon into so gay and lightsome a one as a butterfly's? I imagine the wise old caterpillars shaking their heads – no, it can't be; it's a fantasy, self-deception, a dream. Similarly, our wise ones. Yet in the limbo between living and dying, as the night clocks tick remorselessly on, and the black sky implacably shows not one single streak or scratch of grey, I hear those words: *I am the resurrection, and the life,* and feel myself to be carried along on a great tide of joy and peace.

Jesus asked Martha whether she believed what he said about being the resurrection and the life. Yes, she believed that he was *the Christ, the Son of God, which should come into the world.* Then she went and told her sister that the Master had arrived and was calling for her. So Mary *arose quickly, and came unto him.* Some of the mourners followed her, supposing that she was going to Lazarus's tomb to weep there. When she saw Jesus she at once fell down at his feet, and said, as Martha had, that, had he been there, then her brother would never have died. It was the sight of Mary weeping, along with those who had accompanied her, that made Jesus finally acquiesce in what was required of him. Troubled in spirit and groaning, he asked where Lazarus was laid, and they told him to come and see. Now he began to weep himself, which made the others marvel at how much he must have loved Lazarus, while some of them asked with a touch of acrimony: Couldn't someone like himself who had *opened the eyes of the blind, have caused that even this man should not have died?* When they arrived at the tomb, which was a cave with a stone in front of it, Jesus asked that the stone should be removed, but the ever-practical Martha protested that by now, four days after Lazarus's death, the corpse would be stinking. Her protest was brushed aside, and Jesus addressed himself to God, offering thanks that he had been heard; adding – for the record, one feels – that of course he knew he would be heard, as he always was, but that in present circumstances, with a large number of people present, he had deliberately stressed the point in order that the glory of God might be made manifest. The stone by this time had been taken away, and Jesus *cried with a loud voice: Lazarus, come forth!* Whereupon Lazarus duly came forth, *bound hand and foot with graveclothes: and his face was bound about with a napkin.* Jesus gave instructions that he should be loosed and allowed to depart – presumably, to go home with his sisters.

What exactly happened? As with the Virgin Birth, a twentieth-century mind recoils from believing that a man can be thus raised from the dead, though ready enough to accept the notion that a life

They took away the stone from the place where the dead was laid.

STONE CARVING, C. 1110

100

can be more or less indefinitely protracted, or even – a project, as I have read, seriously entertained in California – that a live body can be frozen for some centuries and then defrosted and resume living. There is, it seems, a whole menagerie of frozen millionaires, male and female, who have established trust funds to finance the maintenance of their stalactitic existence, with instructions that at a propitious moment they shall be thawed out for another spell of active life. Various elucidations of the raising of Lazarus have been proffered, calculated to bring the episode more into line with contemporary attitudes. For instance, that Lazarus's death was moral rather than physical, resulting from some appalling sin he had been led into committing, and that the miracle Jesus performed was to bring him back to moral sanity.

In any case, the account in the Fourth Gospel is quite specific; Jesus brought a man who had been dead four days back to life, and the mere report of such a happening, as may readily be believed, made Jesus so notorious, and so scared the Jewish authorities because of the excitement liable to be caused among the populace, that they finally made up their minds by one means or another to bring about Jesus's death. If we let him alone, they reasoned, *all men will believe on him: and the Romans shall come and take away both our place and nation*. It was Caiaphas, that year's High Priest, who put the matter bluntly. Better, he argued, that one man should die than the whole nation perish. It is the argument commonly used to justify the execution of martyrs, but in this case Caiaphas spoke truer than he knew, for Jesus's death was to save, not just a nation, but all mankind. Thenceforth, we are told, the High Priest and his associates took counsel together as to how they might best arrange for Jesus to be killed.

Jesus's ministry was now drawing to a close. In worldly terms it could scarcely be regarded as successful. For some two years he had been going about through *every city and village, preaching and showing the glad tidings of the Kingdom of God*. His miracles had made a stir, certainly, and we are told that people flocked to hear him. He had his twelve disciples, who had been sent out to preach and heal on their own account. As healers they were not always successful; in a particular case, though specifically given authority over evil spirits or demons, they had notably failed to dislodge one, to Jesus's great displeasure. If they had prayed more, he told them, and their faith had been stronger, they would have succeeded. How widely Jesus had become known is difficult to judge. The Gospels, very naturally, imply that his words and miracles were on everyone's lips, but it is significant that Pilate had never heard of Jesus when he was brought before him, even though it was his business to keep track of agitators and wandering evangelists liable to stir up the excitable populace in his turbulent province.

Jesus had no organization, no headed notepaper, no funds, no registered premises, no distinguished patrons or officers, except only a treasurer – the ill-famed Judas Iscariot. When the disciples were sent out they were instructed to take with them no money or food, neither staff nor spare clothes; to make no arrangements or plans of any kind, but just to look for hospitality where they could find it, and if none were forthcoming, depart, shaking the dust off their feet by way of a testimony. In consequence, Jesus assured them, that particular place would fare worse on the day of judgment than Sodom or Gomorrah. It may be assumed that Jesus followed the same practice, and that when he said the Son of Man had nowhere to lay his head, it was literally the case. He, too, just went from place to place, speaking, healing, finding food and shelter where he might.

One thing I know, that, whereas I was blind, now I see.

ILLUSTRATION FROM THE EVANGELIARY OF OTTO III

There was nothing written down, no membership forms or minutes of the last meeting; no badges even, until, with his death, he gave the world the greatest badge ever known – the Cross. No halls were hired, as St Paul did in Ephesus; except for occasional social gatherings, and, of course, the momentous Last Supper, everything would appear to have happened in the open air. For me, it is a reminiscence of Jesus when I catch a glimpse of a lonely orator holding forth, say, in Lincoln's Inn Fields, on some theme or other – as it might be, proportional representation, or the imminent end of the world. This, more than High Mass in St Peter's, or the consecration of a new Archbishop of Canterbury, conveys the image of Jesus proclaiming the coming of his Kingdom. Listeners are few – a faithful follower or two, part of the speaker's *équipe*; some passers-by briefly pausing, an occasional stray dog. Yet how extraordinary if once again a new era were being ushered in, signalized by the coming of another Kingdom and another Saviour! Just to be on the safe side, I edge nearer and listen. Quite often new eras and last days *are* being proclaimed, but so far I have not come across another Saviour.

How small a band they were! And how small the distances covered in their journeyings! Repeating the same words, re-enacting the same scenes; the sick gathering and crying out, the blind for their sight, the halt for their limbs, the lepers for uncontaminated flesh. Such itinerant *exaltés* usually manage to make a stir. Even in our own time the Maharishis flourish, the self-styled prophets multiply, the soothsayers who claim to have all the answers find enough support to print and circulate their nostrums. In cities like New York fortune-tellers are as numerous as psychiatrists, and star-gazers provide popular and lucrative newspaper and magazine features. The wilderness is large, and there are always many voices crying in it.

This particular itinerant *exalté*, alone of them all, made the preposterous claim that he was God's only begotten Son, and what is more, the claim was accepted; not just by others as crazy as himself, but by the master-minds and hearts of a great civilization, into whose art and law and literature and learning it was to be indelibly written. At the time, a paltry affair; in the end, to prove the greatest affair ever enacted. Our contemporary Media captains may marvel at the astonishing result of so insignificant a beginning, imagining to themselves what they would have made of the opportunity; the lavish presentations they would have mounted, his words carried by satellite to every corner of the globe, his Kingdom presented at prime time in living colour to hundreds of millions of viewers of every race and nationality; the very Second Coming itself appropriately simulated, with a Jesus riding in on clouds of glory as a super-super-super-star. Who then, would have been able to resist him? The late Lord Beaverbrook, in his book on the subject (*The Divine Propagandist*), sees in Jesus a propagandist of stupendous possibilities, provided, of course, that all the nonsensical notions about him, as a Man of Sorrows who took a poor view of riches and advocated crazy practices like loving our enemies, are put aside. Suitably sub-edited, Beaverbrook claimed, the New Testament might yet prove a circulation builder.

In addition to the healing and the fulfilment of his Messiahship, and the mysterious apocalyptic sayings that went therewith, capable of baffling those who heard them at the time as well as those who have brooded upon them subsequently, Jesus had things to say about how we should behave which captivated his listeners, and have continued to captivate succeeding generations. This is not because the standards he proposed were lax and easy-going, like today's permissiveness. Far from it. They asked more of his followers than any other teacher ever has – to do good to those who harm us, and pray for those who persecute us; when we are struck on the right cheek to turn to the smiter the other cheek also, and when someone has taken our coat to hand over our cloak; to give to whoever asks, and lend to whoever would borrow, and when someone presses us to go with him one mile, to go with him two. Not just to refrain from adultery, but to refrain from desiring, which amounts to the same thing, and not just to refrain from killing, but from being angry or calling someone a fool, these being also mortal sins – alas!

No less startlingly contrary to what passes for being human nature are the Beatitudes, enunciated by Jesus in his famous Sermon on the Mount, which, according to the Gospels, was delivered to his disciples from a hill-top where he had taken refuge from the press of people who, with many sick among them, had gathered round him. It is quite possible, however, that they never were delivered as a single sermon, but represent a collection of Jesus's most characteristic utterances on the subject of human behaviour for the convenience of the early churches. Either way, they are sublime, and have been woven into the very texture of the Christian era's thought and moral and spiritual aspiration.

What the Beatitudes say is that the poor, not the rich, are blessed; that the meek, not the strong, inherit the earth; that the merciful obtain mercy, the pure in heart see God, and Heaven belongs to those who are persecuted for righteousness' sake. Jesus was the sweetest of all moralists in that he formulated no code and invoked no earthly sanctions. The punishments and rewards, if there were any, would be in Heaven and Hell; the dynamic of his morality was love, not law, and its realization in Eternity, not in Time. None the less, there had to be law; and Jesus insisted that he had not come to destroy but to fulfil it. Not one jot or tittle, he said, would pass away until the whole destiny of man had been accomplished. Without law there can be no order, and without order no virtue, but law is the measure of our human imperfection, as virtue is its image. Or, put another way, law and virtue are two sticks on which we hobble along despite our mortal infirmities, when otherwise, like Bunyan's Pilgrim, we should sink without trace in the Slough of Despond or perish at the hands of the Giant Despair. Nor is it the case, as Jesus tells us, that because he has superseded the Law, as his followers we can do whatever we have a mind to. On the contrary, our standards have to be, not more lax, but even stricter than those of the Law. Thus, if the Law allows divorce for adultery, that is only out of consideration for the frailties of men; a concession almost contemptuously granted. In the eyes of God, Jesus insists, a man and a woman who marry become one flesh; God has joined them together, and no human agency should be allowed to part them asunder. For true Christians, the bond between a husband and wife can never be broken, as their love can never depend on their bodily union. The body is only the book in which love's mysteries are written; they grow in souls and are harvested in Eternity. In the early days of the Church the Apostle Paul had to set his face strongly against the notion that, under the dispensation of Jesus, his followers could do what they liked – the more so because, as they might reason, the world was soon to end, so what did it matter anyway? *The flesh lusteth against the Spirit, and the Spirit against the flesh*, Paul insisted to the Christians in Galatia, *and these are contrary the one to the other: so that ye cannot do the things that ye would.* Significantly enough, it was Luther's favourite text.

Did Jesus mean, then, that we should take his sublime moral propositions as mere beautiful aspirations: to be admired, and even adored, but not practised? This is the view of men of action, who smile rather pityingly at the notion of loving our enemies and doing good to those who harm us. Or, worse, who insist that their own fell purposes are an expression of these very propositions; so that they love their enemies by dive-bombing them, or do good to those who harm them by handing them over to firing-squads, or assassinating them, or otherwise procuring their disappearance. I discussed this once with Enoch Powell, the two of us standing in twin pulpits in the Church of St Mary-le-Bow in London's Cheapside. Our theme

Go, and sin no more.

MOSAIC, C. 1185

was God and Caesar; the arc-lights had been installed, and the cameras – Caesar's eyes keeping us under surveillance – were rolling. To Powell it was quite clear that no one – certainly no one engaged in politics – could literally follow Jesus's precepts of loving his enemies and doing good to those who harmed him. It would bring the Government down, and induce other even worse disasters. How could you be expected, as Leader of the Opposition, say, to love the Prime Minister? Or vice versa? Or to do good to an Honourable Member who moved an awkward amendment? Such precepts were not meant to be put into practice, and to suppose otherwise was merely humbug; in any case, ridiculous. A religious with no stake in any human society, no wife, no children, no domestic or social responsibilities, might live in accordance with the precepts in the Sermon on the Mount. Thomas à Kempis, yes; but then he was not Member of Parliament for Wolverhampton SW. As Powell was speaking, with the arc-lights shining down, and Caesar's eyes fixed steadily on him, it seemed to me that his black suit turned into a cowl, and that a tonsure disclosed itself on the crown of his neatly brushed head. How easily he might have been a monk instead of a politician, his eyes blazing and his voice rising in the service of God, as now in the service of Caesar! The two services in their extremities meet. After all, Jesus himself, while calling on us to love and be considerate towards our enemies, could angrily denounce his, the Pharisees, as *whited sepulchres, which indeed appear beautiful outward, but are within full of dead men's bones*, as *ye serpents, ye generation of vipers, how can ye escape the damnation of hell?* Such inconsistencies are, perhaps, a special mercy for those of us, weaker brethren, among his followers, with an incurable love for such barbed words.

Contrasting with Powell's position is that of the extreme pacifist, as taken by a Gandhi, or, for that matter, a Tolstoy. As advocates of non-violence in accordance with Jesus's principle of turning the other cheek and returning good for evil, they considered it to be possible to contract out of the coercion on which all human societies are based, while still enjoying the security of person and property the Law, as enforced by the police and other organs of power, provides. In the case, particularly, of Gandhi, who found himself leader of the Swaraj movement in a political struggle for Indian independence, the intrinsic contradictions became all too apparent. Professing non-violence, he indirectly stirred up much violence, before, during and after the achievement of Indian self-government, and he died by an assassin's hand deeply disillusioned with the results of the independence he had been largely instrumental in achieving. If Jesus had been lured into similarly associating himself with the Zealots, or Jewish nationalists, he would have found himself in the same case as Gandhi, who has now lost all the glory of being a great moral teacher, and become merely the symbol of a dying and deeply corrupt political movement.

Jesus's subsequent followers have been less careful. They have sent him on Crusades, made him a freedom-fighter, involved him in civil wars and conspiracies, sent him picketing and striking and leading cavalry charges, and finally made him a paid-up member of the British Labour Party, with the strong expectation that in due course he will be given a life peerage and take his place in the House of Lords. In the light of these aberrations I have sometimes asked myself how Jesus would have fared if he had been born into one of the points of conflict in our world as Galilee was in his – in South Africa, say. As a white South African he would assuredly have been killed by his fellow whites for insisting that they should love and serve their black fellow citizens; as a black South African, he would likewise have been killed by his fellow blacks for telling them they must love and serve their white oppressors. In neither case, it is safe to assume, would he have been a beneficiary under the World Council of Churches' munificence in providing financial support for African guerrillas aiming to achieve national independence by means of terrorism.

Though, in the Sermon on the Mount and other discourses, Jesus proclaimed the loftiest moral standards the world has ever heard, at other times he would take a severely practical view of human be-haviour and the ethical attitudes that go therewith. In the parable of the talents, for instance, the servant who failed to invest money entrusted to him is severely blamed on the ground that, as he admittedly knew his master to be a hard man, *taking up that* [*he*] *had laid not down and reaping that* [*he*] *did not sow*, he should have acted accordingly. Whereas the other servants who invested the money are allowed to keep it along with the increment earned, this one loses even what he had so carefully hoarded, and is cursed into the bargain as a wicked as well as a stupid servant; the moral being *that unto everyone which hath shall be given; and from him that hath not, even that he hath shall be taken away from him.* It is a hard saying, but who can deny that it is true to the ways of the world? Again, on another occasion an unjust steward is praised as having acted prudently when, under notice of dismissal, he ingratiates himself with his master's creditors by writing down their liabilities. It is – putting it mildly – sharp practice, but none the less commended on the ground that we need to make friends of the mammon of unrighteousness.

*Blessed are the poor in
spirit : for theirs is the
kingdom of heaven.*

PART OF BRONZE DOOR,
BENEVENTO CATHEDRAL

For the children of this world are in their generation wiser than the children of light – in other words, those who are active participants in the world of money and power will understand its workings much better than those who, being followers of Jesus, are living in terms of quite different values and seeking quite different ends.

Jesus was not, in our contemporary sense, an idealist, and gives no intimation of believing that the world could be made better on its own terms, any more than that individual human beings could make themselves better on their own terms. Just as they needed to be reborn, so the world would be reborn with the coming of God's Kingdom. Jesus came among us precisely to show how men could be reborn, and to proclaim the coming of the Kingdom, whose final realization might be expected when history ended; an eventuality whose precise timing could not be known in advance, so everyone should live in a perpetual state of readiness for it. Otherwise, we had to accept the world as it was, recognizing that the *children of this world*, the Herods and the Pilates and the Caiaphases, would never be induced to function on a basis of Jesus's Beatitudes. Nor should Jesus's own *children of light* expect to be as wise in their generation as the others. Rather, they must take stock of the mammon of unrighteousness; for otherwise, *Who will commit to your trust the true riches?* To understand the conduct of this world's affairs, that is to say, we must look to the experts – the Machiavellis, the de Tocquevilles, the Swifts – thereby qualifying for initiation into celestial *realpolitik* where Jesus's principles prevail. In the same sort of way, a clean window helps us to look more clearly into Eternity, and a good time-keeper to attune ourselves the better to the exigencies of everlasting life.

I cannot see that Jesus ever advocated a reform of any kind, or supported any human cause, however enlightened. His teaching ranged between the sublimest mysticism and the bluntest realism, leaving out the middle-ground, the lush pastures of liberalism and goodwill, where editorialists and Media pundits graze, and a stifling sirocco wind of rhetoric endlessly blows. He gave us, not a plan of action, nor even a code of ethics, certainly not a programme of reforms, but those wonderfully illuminating contradictions of his – the first to be the last, the poorest the richest, the weakest the strongest, the most obscure the most celebrated. He silenced the stridency of the ego, freed the elbows and unharnessed the shoulders from their urge to push and shove, abated the will's rage and the flesh's obduracy. The meek, he told us, would inherit the earth, and he showed us how to be meek, humility being the very condition of virtue. Then, along with this heavenly roller-coaster ride whose tickets are only available for those who cannot pay, there is the hard, gritty, abject wisdom of the world, also with its own kind of appeal, and even charm, especially as conveyed in Jesus's parables. For instance, the labourers in the vineyard, early trade unionists, who grumbled because, when they received their contractual wage, they found that others who had come later on to the job were being paid the same amount. Or the children in the market-place whom there was no pleasing; to piping they would not dance, and to wailing they would not mourn. Or the prodigal son who, having wasted his patrimony on riotous living, returned home broken and penitent, only to find his father had prepared a great feast in his honour, to the understandable fury of his virtuous brother. Or the man who, coming late at night to borrow some bread from a friend, is told for his pains: *Trouble me not : the door is now shut, and my children are with me in bed; I cannot rise and give thee*; but who still goes on asking, until at last the other does rise and give him as many loaves as he wants, not because they are friends, but because of his importunity, the moral being: *Ask, and it shall be given you; seek, and ye shall find; knock, and it shall be opened unto you* – words of rare comfort. Or the leaven that is like the Kingdom of Heaven because it makes the soggy dough rise, to become light crusty bread. Or the light that is not to be put under a bushel but on a candlestick, so that *it giveth light unto all that are in the house*. Or the merchantman in search of goodly pearls who, when he found one of great price, *went and sold all that he had, and bought it*. Or the man with a hundred sheep who, when one of them has gone astray, goes after that one, and when he has found it, *rejoiceth more of that sheep, than the ninety and nine that went not astray*.

This practical wisdom in Jesus's parables cannot be faulted. Through all history's changes, the revolutions and counter-revolutions, the rise and fall of great ones, it has continued to be valid. Take, for instance, what he tells us about money; a key matter at all times and in all circumstances. In the first place, there is his statement that the poor are blessed. Today, this amounts to blasphemy. Set up in type, it will positively melt the lead; pronounced in a television studio, it will cause a deathly hush, making the lights go out, the floor-manager drop dead, and the Director-General hurriedly issue an apology that so monstrous a perversion of truth should have been uttered on the air. The poor blessed! How in God's name can that be? It is a denial of our whole way of life; a contradiction of everything we believe in, of every single advertisement transmitted on every TV channel, or alluringly set forth in print and colour; of everything said by every single politician and demagogue, of the contentions of every party and ideology. All of these say: Get rich and be happy. Riches bring everything desirable – travel, speed, the delights of love and every human bliss. How beautiful are the bodies of the rich as they run, laughing, into the sea! Or as they sit at the wheel of a fast car, or look at one another's perfection across a white table-cloth beside the blue Mediterranean, Gatsby-like in their whiteness and fragrance and freshness! Who in his senses could suppose that the opposite state – poverty – is to be preferred? Poverty, as Bernard Shaw vehemently insisted, is dirty, squalid, unmanicured and ungroomed; not just unblessed, but a fall from grace, a sinful condition imposed by a cruel and unjust social system. Yet Jesus dared to say that the poor were blessed, and what is more, through the centuries the choicest spirits have not just agreed with him, but often, in order to participate in this blessedness, embraced poverty themselves in its extremist form. As blissful at being naked on the naked earth as others are at being tucked up in newly laundered linen sheets; as joyous in their lack of possessions as others are in their yachts, their convertibles, their swimming-pools.

With us, affluence is a religion. Supermarkets celebrate it – buy this in remembrance of me! Banks are its holy of holies – spend this in remembrance of me! The television studios are chapels-of-ease. I sat in one once with Mother Teresa in New York while she was questioned by a man in a mauve shirt with a drooping green moustache and sad eyes peering out through thick spectacle lenses. Every minute or so he broke off for a commercial. That morning they happened all to be recommending different packaged foods as being neither fattening nor even nourishing. Mother Teresa, thinking no doubt of the human skeletons she tried to clothe in a little flesh, listened with a kind of wonder, and then, in her soft but clearly audible voice, broke in to remark: 'I see that Christ is needed in television studios.' Everyone heard her, and a strange silence descended on the studio. I half expected an enraged figure to appear, rope in hand, as he had at the Temple of Jerusalem, to drive us all out into the street. On the previous occasion it was the money-changers; today, the advertisers. Surely he would come, eyes ablaze: You bastards! You and your guaranteed unnourishing bread! In the event, he did not come, but Mother Teresa's words about Christ being needed in television studios, I am sure, continued to echo in the hearts of all who heard them, perhaps serving a similar purpose. In his humanity, Jesus, like Swift, knew what it was to feel furious indignation lascerating his heart, and in the heat of it beat up the money-changers going about their lawful occasions; just as in his divinity he could tell us that the poor, their chief victims, were blessed. The writers of the Gospels, very creditably, evince no inclination to apologize for Jesus's humanity; nor, for that matter, to accentuate unduly his divinity. The Son of Man loses his temper, as sons of men do, while the Son of God keeps his, making us understand that the poor veritably are blessed, and the Kingdom of God theirs.

Then there is the case of the rich man, or ruler, who came to Jesus and, addressing him as *Good Master*, asked him what he could do to inherit eternal life. Was it a try-on? Or did he really want to know? I should suppose something between the two; that he was curious about Jesus, and anxious to find out what manner of man he was. So, he put to him a typical television interviewing question, designed, equally, to probe and to elucidate. Seated in the studio, knee to knee, the lights on, the boom-mike falling to within biting distance. Now – Action! Your Eminence, Your Grace, or just plain Bishop, 'what must we do to inherit eternal life?' Quite a stunner in its way, when he was all ready for: 'Why do you think the churches are emptying?' Or: 'How do you feel about the present thrust to ecumenism?' Hm, what was that? – why, yes, of course. . . . As though he had been asked whether he believed in monogamy, or disbelieved in apartheid. Jesus was obviously irritated by being addressed as *Good Master*. Why do you call me good?, he snapped. *There is none good but one, that is God.* Then, not giving the ruler time to respond to this rebuke, he goes on: *Thou knowest the commandments. Do not kill. Do not steal. Do not bear false witness. . . . Honour thy father and thy mother.* Yes, the ruler knew the commandments well, and, as a matter of fact, had kept them from his youth up. They are, after all, relatively easy to keep, especially if, as an Anglican bishop once suggested, they are regarded as an examination paper, with eight only to be attempted. At this point Jesus begins to love the man; you can see it coming on. He always ends by loving everyone – the woman of Samaria; little Zacchaeus, the villainous tax-gatherer lurking in the branches of a tree he had climbed to get a better view of Jesus, who, when he spotted him, mischievously called him down, and invited himself to dinner. (Who can invent such things? They have to be true.) Even Judas, who went so dolefully off to collect his money – a doleful enough errand for all of us; even his enemies who had nailed him on the Cross, the two-faced High Priest, feeble Pilate and cunning Herod, the sycophantic Sanhedrin men, the lordly Scribes and Pharisees, the yelling mob and the ribald soldiers, all, all, loved, and to be forgiven, *for they know not what they do.* It is our best hope;

He saw a man, named Matthew, sitting at the receipt of custom : and he saith unto him, Follow me.

PAINTING BY VAN ROYMERSWAELE

114

I cling to it – that we know not what we do, even though we do know, perfectly well.

Jesus listened to the ruler's declaration of virtue, and then came the devastating remark, in a similar vein to the one to Martha: *Yet lackest thou one thing : sell all that thou hast, and distribute unto the poor, and thou shalt have treasure in heaven.* Jesus had a way of thus probing into the very soul. The ruler might just have managed to dispose of his possessions, great as they were, possibly working out some sort of charitable trust; house and gardens handed over to the public, with himself as custodian. It was the concluding words that were too much for him. Disposing of all his worldly goods was not the end of it; when that had been done there was the same call as to the disciples: *Come, follow me.* Matthew got up from his seat at the receipt of custom; the fishermen left their boats and their nets, took no luggage, said no goodbyes, but went lumbering after their Master, who had promised them, with his familiar touch of irony, that thenceforth they would be catching, not fish, but men. For the ruler it was too much to ask; *when he heard this he was very sorrowful, for he was very rich.* Such superb pay-off lines occur quite often in the New Testament; perhaps the most devastating of all being St Paul's comment on a lost friend: *For Demas hath forsaken me, having loved this present world.* The ruler is heard of no more. What were his feelings, I wonder, at the time of the Crucifixion. Perhaps by that time he had forgotten his encounter with Jesus, married a new wife, appeared on television, become concerned about pollution of the environment and the population explosion.

After the ruler had gone Jesus remarked on how difficult it is for the rich to enter into the Kingdom of God, using a comparison to illustrate his point that has become famous – that it is easier for a camel to go through the eye of a needle than for a rich man to get to Heaven. Has any single sentence in the New Testament been more mulled over than this one? If Jesus's statement is to be taken at its face value, then riches become, not merely, a dubious benefit, but positively disastrous. To rub in the point, there is the awful example of the beggar Lazarus, who sat miserably at a rich man's gate, and then went to Heaven, while the rich man in due course found himself roasting in Hell. From there he saw Lazarus resting on Abraham's bosom, but his appeals across the impassable gulf that lies between Heaven and Hell proved fruitless. Abraham told him that there was no way of helping him, and that he should remember how *thou in thy lifetime receivedst thy good things, and likewise Lazarus evil things; but now he is comforted, and thou art tormented.* More worldly wisdom,

There was a certain rich man, which was clothed in purple and fine linen, and fared sumptuously every day : And there was a certain beggar named Lazarus, which was laid at his gate, full of sores.

PAINTING ON PANEL, FIFTEENTH CENTURY

and a bleak prospect for the rich! To mitigate their fate the help of Biblical scholarship has been invoked, and the suggestion made that the eye of a needle to which Jesus referred was the name of one of the gates into Jerusalem; this gate being rather a tight squeeze for a camel to get through, especially if heavily loaded. No one need have worried; Jesus's sombre account of the poor prospects for the rich in the hereafter do not appear to have seriously diminished in this world the lure of riches, which have continued to be avidly sought after despite the eye of the needle and what happened to Lazarus. The disciples clearly took Jesus's comment on his encounter with the ruler quite literally, and asked him whether it meant that there would be no rich men in Heaven – an eventuality they could doubtless face with equanimity. In purely human terms, this would be so, Jesus told them, but *the things which are impossible with men are possible with God.* It is the built-in proviso to all our presumptions. We can never be sure that anything is impossible, or for that matter, possible. God is the divine joker in our pack.

The real worry of the disciples was not about whether or not the rich man would get to Heaven, but about their own chances. Here, Jesus saw fit to reassure them. No one, he said, who had left his home and his family for the sake of the Kingdom of God but would receive more than his deserts in this world, and in the world to come everlasting life. Even then they continued to fret, and on another occasion asked Jesus who among them might have the privilege in Paradise of sitting on either side of him. On this point Jesus refused to be drawn, and said – another of the times when I imagine a twinkle in his eye – that such decisions on heavenly *placement* rest with God alone. The disciples were often quarrelsome and envious and cowardly; it is extraordinary what Jesus made of them – as though calculating that to found a universal religion, a church and a civilization out of such poor material would redound to God's greater glory. Very occasionally, he lost his temper with them; as when they were terrified while out in their boat during a storm on the Lake of Galilee, and came and woke him up, whereupon he *rebuked the winds and the sea; and there was a great calm.* Or when he warned them against the leaven of the Pharisees and Sadducees, and they obtusely took him to be referring to their having run out of bread. Mostly, however, he was loving and considerate even when they failed him. There was, for instance, the occasion when the three disciples who had accompanied him to the Garden of Gethsemane fell asleep while he was praying, instead of keeping watch as he had asked. I see him looking at them as they lay on the ground, with the poignant abandonment

of sleeping men (something I remember so well from barrack-hut days), mouths open, heads thrown back, features relaxed, limbs limp and inert. So vulnerable, so fragile, *What, could ye not watch with me one hour*? Alas, no, not even that – looking at them as God has looked at His creatures through the aeons; disappointment without end weighed against inexhaustible love.

Jesus appears not to have carried money with him ever. When he wanted to make his point about paying tribute to Caesar he called for a coin, presumably not having one himself. Equally, when he and the disciples were in Capernaum, and the question arose of paying the Temple tax – to which all Jews over nineteen were liable – he instructed

The spirit indeed is willing, but the flesh is weak.

PAINTING BY WOLF HUBER

Peter to go down to the Lake of Galilee, throw a line, and he would find that the first fish to bite had a coin in its mouth which would meet the tax for both of them. A Temple tax-collector, as some sort of a try-on, had approached Peter and asked him whether or not his Master paid the half-shekel due from him annually for Temple maintenance. Doubtless to avoid possible trouble, Peter said that he did. Later, Jesus with mock solemnity argued that he was not, in fact, liable. God's particular family, he insisted, should not be required to contribute towards the upkeep of His home. That was for outsiders. It was a thin argument, and the instruction to Peter none the less to pay the tax, getting the money out of a fish's mouth, suitably rounded it off. Significantly, there is no word in the Gospels of Peter actually carrying out Jesus's instructions and going to the Lake with his line. Galilee fishermen to this day show one the fish in question; a little fish with special rusty markings round its mouth. Somehow, when I was shown one, I found it very touching; the miraculous and the ordinary rub shoulders very charmingly, like sensuality and adoration in human love.

Credo quia impossibile is a wonderful saying. The more unlikely the miracle, the easier to believe; only the concrete and the factual invites scepticism. Compared with such banal statements as that two plus two equals four, or that nature abhors a vacuum, looking for the wherewithal to pay the Temple tax in a fish's mouth seems a delectable enterprise. In euphoric moments only the impossible will do. Thus, lovers instinctively turn to the miraculous to convey what they feel. In the same sort of way, in ages of faith the builders of churches drive their steeples recklessly into the sky. 'Give me a man in love', says St Augustine. 'Give me one who yearns; give me one who is hungry; give me one far away in the desert who is thirsty and sighs for the spring of the Eternal. Give me that sort of man; he knows what I mean.' It was his love relationship with men which enabled Jesus to perform his miracles, and our love relationship with him that enables us to believe in them. Jesus compared a grain of seed, a tiny speck in the palm of his hand, to the Kingdom of Heaven. What a ridiculous comparison it would seem in the eyes of anyone who did not know what a seed is and what it can become! In point of fact, is there anything more miraculous in the universe? That tiny speck, planted in the earth, decomposing there, under the same necessity as we are to die in order to be reborn; then putting out shoots, becoming an ear of corn, a flower more gloriously attired than Solomon, a tree even, with birds nesting in its branches. Containing within its minute self all the mysterious potential of creation. No wonder Jesus compared it to the Kingdom of Heaven! No microscope however powerful, or computer analysis of seeds, their cultivation and crop-potential, helps us to understand the comparison; but down on our knees, full of the foolishness of love, straining after that light Jesus brought into the world, it becomes clear.

Though Jesus had no money himself, there were funds at his and the disciples' disposal, presumably contributed by wellwishers. Judas Iscariot looked after this money. Jesus insisted from the beginning that the service of mammon was not compatible with God's; one or the other had to be chosen. Love of money constituted a servitude, for *where your treasure is, there will your heart be also.* Giving money away should be secret, the left hand not knowing what the right one is doing. Jesus contrasted the ostentatious alms of the Pharisees with the widow's mite, which meant so much more to her than their lavish offering because it was her all. In other words, money has no intrinsic value, but only a relative one; the widow's mite was, in this sense, literally more than the Pharisees' munificence. The doom of the rich was to believe in their riches; like the man who stocked up his barns and storehouses with his crops' abundance, and thought then to settle down to eat, drink and be merry, only to have his soul required of him that very night. So, we should not lay up for ourselves *treasures upon earth, where moth and rust doth corrupt, and where thieves break through and steal.* The only lasting treasure is spiritual, as the only perfect freedom is serving God.

All these maxims have been piously quoted and believed through the centuries, but none the less the love of money continues to be, as St Paul wrote to Timothy, *the root of all evil: which while some coveted after, they have erred from the faith, and pierced themselves through with many sorrows.* There are no recorded cases of men being made happy by money, and yet they continue to respond to its allure. Jesus knew this and took due account of it; on the one hand, recognizing that the mammon of unrighteousness was an inescapable factor in human life, and on the other preparing the way for the great love-affairs with poverty of Christians like St Francis which have revealed the startling beauties of austerity, the fabulous riches of deprivation, the sheer abundance and variety that the life of the spirit offers when it has been pruned of all the dead wood, sterile blooms and parasitic growths that carnality accumulates. In these terms Christians have sought poverty as ardently as any gold-prospector his pay-dirt. Likewise chastity, which offers ecstasies as far transcending those of the flesh as Donne's poem 'The Ecstacy' transcends *Fanny Hill.* Jesus did not just ask us to control our cupidity and sensual appetites; he generated a no less ardent propulsion in the opposite direction, as the life force operating in the growth of trees and plants and all vegetation opposes the force of gravity – one pushing upwards and outwards and the other pulling downwards. At his instance, sated, we pine for abstinence, and stifling in the labyrinthine maze of sex, for chastity. Not to flee the world but to discover the world is Jesus's directive; and, once so found, and seen with his eyes, it has depths and splendours hitherto unnoticed – as a pretty face touched with affliction discloses its hidden beauty. If an eye offends pluck it out, Jesus counsels, not thereby becoming blind, but truly seeing; if a limb, amputate it, not thereby becoming crippled, but whole. He came, he tells us, not to destroy life but that we may have it more abundantly. When abundance means the Dead Sea fruit of affluence, this saying is difficult to understand: yet I can say that I never knew what joy was until I gave up pursuing happiness, or cared to live until I chose to die. For these two discoveries I am beholden to Jesus.

So all earthly joys, even the homely ones of human love and work and companionship, pale into insignificance compared with this other joy that Jesus pre-eminently brought into the world, of escaping into reality from the fantasies of the will and the appetites where everything is upside-down and the wrong way round, the good wan and unwanted, the wicked pulsating and desirable, beauty a tired ghost, ugliness sparkling and alive. By contrast, in reality it is goodness that shines with a clear light, and evil that is dark and malodorous, while the present is sufficient unto itself only because it is the intersection of a horizontal and a perpendicular infinitude. In the light of contemporary attitudes, it must seem extraordinary that so much joy could have come of Jesus's seemingly harsh exigencies, whereas the return to pagan permissiveness has spread a dreadful gloom and boredom over the Western World. Does Scandinavia ring with happy laughter? Are the bearded and bra-less communards of California wreathed in smiles and given to dancing through the valleys wild? Do the campuses resound with joyous songs and sparkling words? Scarcely. It is something I have experienced, but cannot explain, that the world renounced glows in all its sounds and shapes and colours as never before; that eyes cast heavenwards catch the texture of flesh, the fold of cloth, the bloom of earthly beauty, as none earthwards bent can hope to attain, and that love seeking no possession, empty-handed, the ego's sting drawn and the blood's fire quenched, shines out like a rising sun filling the universe with warmth and light and rapture.

When Jesus was in Bethany with Lazarus and Martha and Mary, shortly before the last Passover in Jerusalem, an incident occurred which, as Jesus himself foresaw, was to become famous *wheresoever this gospel [is] preached throughout the whole world*. While Martha was preparing supper, Mary took *a pound of ointment of spikenard, very costly, and anointed the feet of Jesus, and wiped his feet with her hair; and the house was filled with the odour of the ointment*. At this Judas, as treasurer, protested, pointing out that the ointment could have been sold for a considerable sum and the money distributed to the poor. It is not at all surprising that the villain among the disciples should appear as the most socially concerned. The wicked are much given to collective moralizing, and the world's worst tyrants – for instance, Napoleon and Stalin and Hitler – usually consider themselves to be humanity's greatest benefactors, while terrorists like Torquemada and Dzerzhinsky and Himmler sanctimoniously see themselves as purifiers rather than destroyers. The position Judas took about Mary's squandering of the ointment on Jesus is precisely the same as that taken today by those who clamour for the sites of city churches and the treasures of the Vatican to be sold and the proceeds given to the poor. If the builders of the city churches and the accumulators of the Vatican treasurers had been of the same opinion, there never would have been any sites or treasures to sell, so we must be thankful that their attitude was more like Jesus's than his betrayer's.

Jesus responded to Judas's criticism by making one of his jokes; Mary, he said, in anointing him, had simply been a little precipitate, and got in ahead of his burial. As it turned out, not very precipitate; just a matter of days. In confuting Judas's criticism of the extravagance involved in anointing him with expensive ointment, Jesus again delivered himself of a remark about the poor – *The poor always ye have with you; but me ye have not always* – which some of his twentieth-century followers have found distressing in its implications. As in the other case – the Beatitude about the poor being blessed – various not very convincing attempts have been made to iron it out into conformity with contemporary attitudes. History, in any case, has vindicated Jesus's observation in the sense that the poor *are* with us still – taking the world scene, just now in ever greater numbers – and are likely to remain so. Again, it is Jesus who has proved the realist, and the believers in an earthly paradise who have been deceived. Pie in the sky may seem illusory, but even more so is pie on the earth.

There are two other versions of the spikenard episode. One, in St Mark's Gospel, sets the scene also in Bethany, but in the house of one Simon the leper, and the ointment is poured over Jesus's head, not his

feet, by an unnamed woman who just appears while they are at dinner. In the other, in St Luke's Gospel, the place is unspecified, and Jesus's host is a Pharisee who has invited him to dinner. A woman of the town, a notorious character, hearing that Jesus is dining at the Pharisee's house, makes her way there, having purchased at considerable expense an *alabaster box of ointment.* Then, standing *at his feet, behind him, weeping [she] began to wet his feet with tears, and did wipe them with the hairs of her head, and kissed his feet, and anointed them with the ointment.* The Pharisee, it may be assumed, in inviting Jesus to his house was actuated more by curiosity than any genuine wish to find out what he had to say; and when he observed the complaisance with which his guest accepted the woman's attentions, he reflected inwardly: *This man, if he were a prophet, would have known who and what manner of woman this is that toucheth him : for she is a sinner* – incidentally, a curious view of prophetic insights. As usual, Jesus knew what he was thinking, and put to him this question: Supposing someone forgave two debts, one of five hundred pence and the other of fifty, which debtor would be the more beholden to him? The Pharisee said he supposed the former. Exactly right. Then

125

Jesus went on to explain the application: when he came into Simon's house no one gave him water for his feet, but the woman wet his feet with her tears and wiped them with her hair. Likewise, no one kissed him, but she had not stopped kissing his feet. Nor did anyone anoint his head with oil, whereas the woman anointed his feet with expensive ointment. *Wherefore I say unto thee, her sins which are many, are forgiven: for she loved much; but to whom little is forgiven, the same loveth little.* Thus Jesus combined a subtle reproach to his host for a certain lack of attentiveness in receiving him, with kinds words to the woman whose sins, he told her, were now forgiven. *Thy faith hath saved thee*, he said to her; *Go in peace*.

Efforts have been made to identify this woman with Mary Magdalene, from whom, we are told, Jesus cast out seven devils. Otherwise, all we know about her is that she belonged to a little company of women – Joanna the wife of Chuza, Herod's steward, and a certain Susanna are named as two others – who followed Jesus, ministering to him and the disciples' needs and contributing to their support. As the centuries have rolled by she has gradually been transformed from a penitent into a heroine, until in the nineteenth century she provided the prototype of the Good Harlot; a sentimentalized figure, dear to second-rate writers like Maupassant and Wilde and Alexandre Dumas *fils*, who comforted themselves by reasoning, fallaciously, that if a whore was dear to Jesus, patronizing whore-houses must be conducive to their and their readers' virtue. In this context, Jesus's remark that *she loved much* is taken as relating to her feelings about her clients rather than to her feelings about Jesus himself, as someone so utterly apart from her own way of life, pursuits and associates, that she was drawn irresistibly to him. Wanting to take something to him that was very precious, she bought for the purpose the expensive ointment with a view to pouring it over his head; but when she found herself actually in his presence, she could only fall at his feet and anoint them with it, bathing them in tears of true penitence and wiping them with her hair in a gesture of true dedication.

The *Boule de Suif*'s and *La Dame aux Camélias*' sentimentalized notions of a harlot belong to fantasy; real whores are often kind and good-natured, as well as lazy and greedy, but by virtue of their very occupation, without love and without sensuality. In the same sort of way, pit ponies are blind and veteran boxers concussed. What Jesus had to give to the Mary Magdalenes was the possibility of loving and feeling, which automatically necessitated their ceasing to be whores. The particular one in question was so grateful for this incomparable

There came a woman having an alabaster box of ointment of spikenard very precious.

PAINTING BY QUENTIN MASSYS

126

gift that she attached herself to Jesus, and we find her among the group of women who were *beholding [the Crucifixion] afar off*, and who helped to prepare Jesus's body for burial by anointing him with spices – for her, the second time, but how different the occasion! And how different was she herself! It was this Mary Magdalene, too, we are told, who in the very early morning after the Crucifixion, while it was still dark, went to the tomb and found it empty; then was the first to see the Risen Lord, whom she mistook for a gardener – an extra glory for an honourable avocation.

That Jesus understood human love in all its connotations, including the sexual, cannot be doubted; otherwise, he would not have been a man. Equally certainly, he was a very attractive person in every way; perhaps especially to women. The contemporary deduction from this would be that either he had sexual relations with women, or that he was frustrated, and therefore unbalanced in his attitude to them. Here, D. H. Lawrence leads the field with his *The Man Who Died*, produced appropriately enough in the intervals of writing and re-writing *Lady Chatterley's Lover*, when he was sick and impotent. The theme, in so far as it can be unravelled, is that Jesus comes to in the tomb after being crucified, hobbles away and encounters Mary Magdalene, to whom he explains that his purpose is no longer to save the world, but only to find fulfilment for himself in the world. She is saddened to find him so changed, and no longer 'the young flamy unphysical exalter of her soul' she had given her heart to, and he feels estranged from her. A young priestess of Isis pleases him better, and becomes pregnant by him – to the best of my knowledge, the only pregnancy in all Lawrence's *œuvre*. In due course, they, too, part. A more ludicrous and complete misunderstanding of the New Testament story – whose whole point is that Jesus is the Man Who Lives – can scarcely be imagined, and one can only say of it, as Dr Johnson said of *Cymbeline*, that 'to remark the folly of the fiction . . . were to waste criticism upon unresisting imbecility'.

Jesus neither discounted our human carnality nor advocated surrender to it. When the Sadducees brought up the far-fetched story of seven brothers who died one after the other, each, in accordance with the Mosaic Law, passing on to the next the same childless wife, and asked to whom this, by that time, one imagines, somewhat battered lady would belong at the Resurrection, Jesus rebuked them with: *When they shall rise from the dead they neither marry, nor are given in marriage; but are as the angels which are in Heaven.* Carnality, in other words, belongs to the world of Time, and in Eternity has no place. Even here, on earth, however, there are some who for one reason or another must eschew carnality – *for there are some eunuchs, which were so born from their mother's womb; and there are eunuchs, which were made eunuchs of men; and there be eunuchs, which made themselves eunuchs for the kingdom of Heaven's sake.* Without a doubt, Jesus saw himself as belonging to the third category, thereby inspiring countless others to take on a life of self-abnegation in the religious orders and otherwise. When I think of all that has been achieved by these dedicated men and women who, like Jesus, have made themselves eunuchs for the Kingdom of Heaven's sake, from exquisite illuminated Missals and Books of Hours, to innumerable good works in the way of looking after the mentally and physically sick, all the scholarship and schools and hospices, all the works of art and literature and mystical insight; not to mention the prayers and devotions which have sweetened and illumined a world given up to egotistic and sensual pursuits – when I think of all this, and even of my own poor efforts to find a similar way, and how immeasurably fuller, happier, more creative life has been to the small degree that I have found it, I marvel that the contemporary view of all such self-abnegation as sick, useless and perverted should seem worthy of a moment's consideration. In any case, there can be no question as to where Jesus stood; *It is the spirit that quickeneth; the flesh profiteth nothing*, he insisted, and though his words can be, and often have been, turned round to signify the opposite of what they say, they still stand, and will for ever.

Jesus himself, even in his obscurity, dreaded the gathering of crowds, and where possible avoided them. Everything in Christianity that matters is from individual to individual; collectivities belong to the Devil, and so easily respond to his persuasion. The Devil is a demagogue and sloganeer; Jesus was, and is, concerned with individual souls, with the Living Word. What he gives us is truth carried on the wings of love, not slogans carried on the thrust of power. It is easy to see why the healing miracles drew people to him and held their attention, but what did they make of his words? Did they relate them to their lives, actually seeking to be pure in heart in order to see God? To forgo laying up treasure on earth, and responding revengefully to wrongs and insults? Or did they suppose, in so far as they considered the matter at all, that Jesus was stating a ludicrously far-fetched ideal with a view to their becoming a little more humane, a little more loving, a little purer of heart, than they would otherwise be? Such has been the prevailing view among the generality of Christians, who are prone to express their love for their enemies by killing them in battle, or encouraging and helping others to ambush and murder them, without feeling that thereby they have infringed Jesus's teaching. Surveying our human scene it is difficult to resist the conclusion that cupidity, vanity, concupiscence and aggressiveness have at all times proved too strong, at any rate in their collective manifestations, to be reversed by Jesus's dynamic of love. So his followers find themselves in the same case as the Pharisees he so roundly abused, who *say and do not* – the worst possible offence.

If, in mortal terms, it may seem ridiculous to expect human beings to turn the other cheek when they are struck, to love their enemies and do good to those who injure them, this does not mean that Jesus's Beatitudes are no more than pious aspirations – visions of a heavenly virtue unattainable on earth. Think of someone in love; he or she is liable to entertain the wildest notions of the felicities which lie ahead. To see the person loved as far more beautiful, chivalrous, considerate, tender and altogether admirable than can ever conceivably be the case, and their life together as far more consistently happy and fruitful than in practice it is likely to be. Yet at the end of the day, if they stay the course, they will look back across the mutually inflicted suffering, the tantrums and rages and jealousies, and see that after all those first dreams of a lasting love – as on Keats's Grecian Urn, for ever warm and still to be enjoyed – have been fulfilled, but not in the way that was expected. The Songs of Innocence echo in the Songs of Experience, and hopes are only irretrievably lost when Time claims the bloom as well as the seed. So with Jesus's Beatitudes, it is as true that enemies will not be loved nor injuries rewarded with kindness as that the world is not a Grecian Urn. Yet still love does not die, and Jesus's Beatitudes, just by virtue of having been spoken by him, have enriched our mortal existence beyond imagining, putting a yeast of love into the unlively dough of human greed and human spite and human wilfulness, so that it can rise marvellously. How inexpressibly wonderful it is, just that the words were uttered all that time ago! How many minds thereby have been uplifted, hearts lightened, souls fired, that would otherwise have found their trough world enough, and its swill all their nourishment.

Jesus summarized all his teaching for us in two great propositions which have provided Christendom with, as it were, its moral and spiritual axis. The first and great commandment, he said, was: *Thou shalt love the Lord thy God with all thy heart, and with all thy soul, and with all thy mind*, and the second, *like unto it : Thou shalt love thy neighbour as thyself*. On these two commandments, he insisted, *hang all the law and the prophets*. His manner of presenting them indicates their interdependence; unless we love God we cannot love our neighbour, and, correspondingly, unless we love our neighbour we cannot love God. Once again, there has to be a balance; Christianity is a system of such balanced obligations – to God and Caesar, to flesh and spirit, to God and our neighbour, and so on. Happy the man who strikes the balance justly; to its imbalance are due most of our miseries and misfortunes, individual as well as collective.

There have been times when the obligation to God pulled too strongly, and the balance had to be redressed in favour of our neighbour. St Simeon Stylites on his pillar most certainly loved God, and would doubtless have claimed to love his neighbour, but perched up there he was too remote for this love to find any effective expression. Gibbon was perhaps right when he wrote of St Simeon that 'such voluntary martyrdom must have gradually destroyed the sensibility both of the mind and the body; nor can it be presumed that the fanatics who torment themselves are susceptible of any lively affection for the rest of mankind.' Had he lived at the time, I feel sure that St Francis, who, in so far as this is possible, achieved a perfect balance between loving God and his neighbour, would have called St Simeon down from his pillar, not to love God less but to love his neighbour more, by joining him and his friars as they went up and down the world's thronging, turbulent highways and byways.

In our own time the balance has swung heavily the other way, and the tendency has been all in the direction of loving our neighbour and forgetting or overlooking God. St Simeon has come down from his pillar to become Comrade Simeon, or the Right Honourable Simeon, or Senator Simeon, or just Sim, with God as no more than a constitutionally elected President to perform ceremonial duties and deliver an annual Speech from the Throne. Deprived of His mystique, God becomes transformed from the Dayspring from on High into one of those Scandinavian monarchs forlornly riding a bicycle about the streets of Stockholm or Copenhagen; addressed in equivalent language with music to match. Worship becomes a seminar, God's House a coffee-bar, and the Word that came to dwell among us full of grace and truth, programmed into People's Logos. Ah, those Jesuit fathers dropping out *shaloms* on all possible occasions, and topping up their chalices with slugs of bourbon, those pipe-smoking Anglican vicars in their leather-patched cassocks ready to dialogue with anyone at the drop of a chasuble, those minute-skirted girls with moon-calf faces peering out of thickets of hair, all agog to be in Bangladesh or among the Katmandu dropouts; good neighbours all, but as for God – well, you have to define your terms. The truth is that the natural, without the supernatural to enrich and enliven it, is too banal to seem to matter much, and only God can turn a neighbour into a brother – which is perhaps what St Paul meant when he wrote of how, *though I bestow all my goods to feed the poor . . . and have not charity, it profiteth me nothing.*

What does loving God mean? We can love the world he created, and the universe which is its setting. We can love all His creatures, including Man, who sees himself as the lord of creation. We can pinpoint our love upon the tiniest instances of life, a flea or a midge, an atom or the particles of an atom. Or expand it to take in the vast eternities of space. We can love paint on canvas, ripe fruit hanging on trees, singing voices, massed masonry, the subtlety and the splendour of words, the rising of the sun in the morning and its setting at nightfall, the grey still twilight of dawn and the golden, murmuring twilight of evening. Likewise a body or a mind at work, straining at some task, and then the sweet relaxation when the work is done, lolling in a chair, eating, to be followed by sleep, stretched out on a bed through the silent night, to awaken, scratching and yawning, to another day. All this we can love, as pertaining to God; but still it is not loving God.

Then again, we may love the godly works of Man. The godly words he tries to utter – though with how much difficulty! – the Cloud of Unknowing into which he ventures, the melodies he makes, the profundities he essays, the laughter he encapsulates – 'That idiot, laughter . . . a passion hateful to my purposes', as Shakespeare's King John calls it, speaking on behalf of all power-maniacs at all times and in all circumstances and places, but for saner souls heard ringing out from Heaven itself, louder sounding when Heaven's gates swing open, abating and dying away as they clang to. All the works of Man, so manifold and wide-ranging – what he builds, what he comes to understand; his explorations of the seen and the unseen, microscopic and universal, as well as into mysteries and meanings; his pyramids, his motorways, his subways and his high-rises, his facts that are fantasies and fantasies that are facts; all the wide range of his quests and curiosities, about himself and his habitat; the dark despair that overwhelms him, and his moments of ecstasy when the doors of the prison of definition are unlocked, and he is free to speak without words and be without being. All this can be loved as emanating from God, and yet not even this is God.

Yet again, there are Man's own particular and private loves, all of which, pertaining to love, partake in some degree of God's love, so that carnality itself, in burning out, leaves ashes which scatter and enrich. Man with his flesh and out of his flesh generating other flesh;

adding his body to another body and making a third comprehending both, blended in such a way that the new creature gives hints of each in little gestures, motions, tricks of speech and ways. How beautiful in old age to note in a grandchild newly born some trait remembered from long ago for its enchantment, and now recurring, like the echo of a distant bell, to bind together an old passion and a new life in one continuing and everlasting chain; a green shoot sprouting from a hollowed-out old tree! Is not this continuity of life, this chain stretching from the first to the last days, something to be loved as God? Most certainly, yet still not God.

How, then, is God Himself, very God of very God, to be found and loved? Not as philosophically conceived, as a First Cause or Categorical Imperative. Though we may, perhaps, come to comprehend, and even cherish, such abstractions, we are not made with a capacity to *love* them. Still less are we capable of loving God as scientifically conceived. Those skulls dug out of some remote Kenyan mountainside, and solemnly captioned and displayed in museums as being so many millions of years old, and the harbingers of Man, may well be possessed of anthropological charisma, but are scarcely, in human terms, lovable. Likewise the humanistic God, the Life Force which has triumphantly carried our species from primeval slime to Professor Ayer, I dare say evokes in some admiration and awe. It would surprise me, however, if this spectacular achievement stirred up in any breast an emotion that could be called love. The simple fact is that to be truly loved God has to become a Man without thereby ceasing to be God. Hence Jesus, who provides the possibility of loving God through, and in, him, and, as part of the same process, of loving other men, our neighbours, through, and in, him. Thus the two commandments become one; to be celebrated in a Man – Jesus – who dies, and sanctified in a Man – also Jesus – who goes on living.

As out of Jesus's affliction came a new sense of God's love, and a new basis for love between men, so out of our affliction we may grasp the splendour of God's love and how to love one another. Thus the consummation of the two commandments was on Golgotha; and the Cross is, at once, their image and their fulfilment. 'It is in affliction itself', Simone Weil writes, 'that the splendour of God's mercy shines; from its very depths, in the heart of its inconsolable bitterness.' We feel ourselves to be forsaken, as Jesus momentarily did on the Cross; and if then we persevere in our love, we end by coming into contact with something which is neither joy nor sorrow, something necessary, pure and essential; something apart from the senses, partaking of both joy and sorrow. Then, at last, triumphantly, we know what it is to love God, and looking outwards from within this love, we see our fellow men, all of them, the sick and the well, the beautiful and the plain, the stupid and the clever, mongols and beauty-queens and imbeciles and athletes, every variety and category of humankind; see them all as brothers and sisters, members of one family, at once enfolded in God's love and chained together by it, as though they were His galley-slaves, and this servitude their perfect freedom.

To bring about this final consummation, Jesus and his little band of followers prepared to make their way to Jerusalem for their last Passover together. His ministry was over; there was nothing more to say or do – except to die. He knew clearly, and the others sensed dimly, that they were approaching the climax of the drama in which they were involved; moving like sleep-walkers towards a predestined end. The disciples had registered a faint protest against going to Jerusalem. *Master, the Jews of late sought to stone thee; and goest thou thither again?* There were twelve hours of daylight, Jesus replied, during which they could walk without stumbling; but when this world's light went out, and night fell, they would stumble unless they had an inner light to guide them. Jesus had this inner light, and it lighted the way to Jerusalem; the city that, as a Jew, Jesus revered, and as the rejected Messiah he pitied and reproached. In his only recorded personal outburst, he cried out at his first glimpse of the city in the distance, set amidst the hills, so strangely and beautifully aloof, as though floating in the sky, and more like a visionary city than an actual one: *O Jerusalem, Jerusalem, thou that killest the prophets, and stonest them which are sent unto thee, how often would I have gathered thy children together, even as a hen gathereth her chickens under her wings, and ye would not!*

PART 3

The Man Who Lives

One short sleep past, we wake eternally,
And death shall be no more, Death thou shalt die.

JOHN DONNE

*If Christ be not risen, then is our preaching vain. . . . If in this
life only we have hope in Christ, we are of all men most miserable.*

I CORINTHIANS 15

Love is such a power that it maketh all things to be shared.
Therefore love Jesus, and all thing that he hath it is thine.
He by his Godhead is maker and giver of time. He by his
Manhood is the true heeder of time. And he by his Godhead
and Manhood together, is the truest judge and the asker of
account of the spending of time. Knit thee therefore to him,
by love and by belief.

THE CLOUD OF UNKNOWING

Many great events have been touched off by very small agencies, but
who could possibly have divined the total redirection of history that
would follow the arrival of thirteen men – Jesus and his twelve
disciples – in Jerusalem for the Feast of the Passover round about
AD 33, in the reign of the Emperor Tiberius? Were the thirteen aware
themselves of the momentousness of the occasion? Jesus certainly
was; in its spiritual, if not its historical, connotation. From the beginning, it had been borne in upon him that the only possible outcome
of the mission on earth God had confided to him was an ignominious
and public death. This was now about to happen, and not just because
it was in the prophecies which he was fated to fulfil. Rather, for the
prophecies' own sake, which would otherwise seem of no account;
and for his own sake, whose sojourn in the world would otherwise be
in vain. Above all, for God's sake, who had ordained that it should be
so. Thus Jesus's death, just as it was to be enacted, on the hill called
Golgotha, between two thieves, the three of them nailed to crosses,
was integral to the drama of his life, and was therefore as inescapable
and at the same time escapable as Socrates' death, or Hamlet's, or
Bonhoeffer's; for that matter, as any death, from a foetus's at the

moment of conception to that of some mindless, rheumy, watery-eyed centenarian who has somehow got overlooked by the humanitarian dispensers of death, the men in white coats making their rounds, dispensing drugs, hypodermic at the ready.

Jesus had to die, and at the same time need not have died as and when he did. The very inevitability of his death made the possibility of his not dying the more actual. Hence his prayer that the cup might yet pass from him; hence the desolating sadness that overwhelmed him in the Garden of Gethsemane; hence his wild cry from the Cross itself asking why God had forsaken him. Every condemned man believes in the possibility of a last-minute reprieve, and yet, when the trapdoor is opened and the noose tightens, when the axe falls, when the current flows through the electric chair, that, too, seems pre-ordained. Similarly, every soldier in a war believes that he will survive, but none the less, when he is hit, and lurches forward, gurgling, blood seeping out him like milk out of an over-fed baby, it is in the sure knowledge that a bullet has been correctly delivered as addressed. So, in the great debate, the ayes and the noes both have it; men are born in chains and are everywhere free to choose what is inexorably decided and decide what is inexorably chosen.

So it must have been with Jesus; he, too, caught in this crossfire, this pincer movement. On the one hand, predestined to suffer and die; on the other, if he so wished, free to live out his life like other men, only occasionally glancing timidly beyond the dimensions of mortality. Seeking the consolations our earthly life offers, such as marrying, and having children, and then grandchildren; growing old, and, as his sight fades, letting his eyes dwell on familiar scenes – the lake, the fishing-boats, the mountains in the distance, and, near at hand, the changing winds and shadows, all the sights and smells and colours he knew so well. Then, when his time comes, dying, with loving, familiar faces gathered round to speed him on his way. Jesus cannot have *wanted* to die so young and so ignominiously. He who described the world so tenderly – the fields white for harvest, the red sky full of promise in the evening and of menace in the morning, the flowers more glorious than Solomon, sorrow turning into joy, as a woman *when she is in travail hath sorrow, because her hour is come : but as soon as she is delivered of the child, she remembereth no more the anguish, for joy that a man is born into the world* – cannot have been ready to take his leave of the world so early. He who understood men and their ways so perfectly, loving them so dearly that he could get inside their skins and restore them to health and sanity, touch their sightless eyes and make them see, soothe their troubled spirits so that

136

they became calm; call them to gather round him like a hen gathering her chickens under her wings, multiply loaves and fishes to stay their hunger, raising them from the grave itself, and calling to him all who travailed and were heavy-laden to give them rest – how could he wish to leave them, like Milton confronted with the prospect of blindness, ere half his days in this dark world and wide were spent?

The temptation must have arisen to leave the prophecies and their splendours, contract out of the stupendous drama in which God had chosen him to be the central character, and settle for the allotted span of three score years and ten like other men. As for his ministry – he could perfectly well cut it short before embarking on that final stretch which led to Golgotha. Turning away from Jerusalem, and returning to Galilee, to grow old there, with all his dreams of the Kingdom of God that he was to usher in, soon becoming a fading memory. He himself something of a local 'character' – pointing at him: 'I've heard tell that when he was young he claimed to be the long-awaited Messiah, and was reputed to have performed miracles. But you know how it is; these things get exaggerated in the telling. Maybe he *did* pull off a spectacular cure or two, though I can't believe that he actually brought someone back from the dead. More likely he managed to sort out a few sufferers from nervous complaints – which can happen. It seems that at the time he attracted quite a following, and caused concern in the Sanhedrin, and even involved the Governor – Pontius something or other. In any case, it all blew over, and now he doesn't talk about it any more; just sits around as the old do, waiting to die. People still think he's a bit, you know, round the bend, but harmless enough, though when the Messiah business was at its height it's said that his family were quite concerned, and thought of having him put away. Now no one bothers. There are always plenty of such crackpots around, anyway.'

It was not to be, of course. Whatever nostalgic thoughts Jesus may have had about staying alive, they could not possibly balance the counter-impulse in him to fall in with God's will, which is the greatest joy available to human beings, and in Jesus's case, in view of his unique relationship with God, his Sonship, more than ever so. What can conceivably equal the sheer delight of doing God's will? For mystics and saints, the highest ecstasy; for the rest of us going about our daily lives, when it happens a source of peace and quietness which nothing else offers. Likewise for all beasts and birds, who in burrowing, scampering, flying, diving, trampling down the thickest jungle, soaring into the sky's highest heights and penetrating the sea's lowest depths, fulfil their own natures, thereby fulfilling God's pur-

137

pose implanted in them. Inanimate things, too, mountains and rocks and stones, which in the shade they give, in their very immobility, perform what God requires of them. As do trees in the fruit they bear, and the wood they make, and the branches and leaves they put out, and plants in their flowers and fragrances, and in the sustenance they provide. Even to doubters and vacillators who waver uncertainly between God and His creatures, inhabiting a wasteland of their own making, muddy and marshy like a river estuary – yes, even to them is vouchsafed very occasionally, just for an instant, a glimpse of God's purpose and their part in it. Coming to them maybe on the wings of a bird, maybe in a note of music or in words strung together, maybe in a beloved face so uniquely familiar that after a million years have passed it stands out among all other faces, instantly and joyously recognizable; but however and whenever it comes, a draught of that living water which does away with all thirsting, a bite of that bread of life after which there is no hungering.

If there is for us this inconceivable happiness, vastly transcending all other kinds, in occasional glimpses of God's purpose and our involvement in it, how much more for Jesus as he came upon Jerusalem, seeing the City, not just as the end of a journey, nor even just as the end of a short life, but as the scene of, at once, a great anguish and a great glory, a great darkness and a great light, a desolating conclusion and a glorious beginning? For him, who had been chosen by God to be, himself, the Paschal Lamb, that *Lamb of God, which taketh away the sin of the world* proclaimed by John the Baptist; to offer himself for sacrifice, not, like Isaac, for one man, his father Abraham, nor for one Chosen People, the Children of Israel, but for all mankind always – what a wonderful fate! Both wonderful and terrible, bringing with it a correspondingly harsh and dreadful joy. Such moments of realized destiny are never simple. Even in the most dedicated they produce a great mixture of emotions, with pride, fear, exaltation, humility, all jostling together. For Jesus it must have been so also. Yet in his case there will have been an ultimate clarity and certainty, enabling him to say, and truly mean: *Not as I will, but as thou wilt.* To be able to say these words and truly mean them is the highest point we can ever hope to attain. Then, indeed, we have broken out of Time's hard shell to breathe, not its stale air, but the fresh, exhilarating atmosphere of Eternity. Jesus achieved this total surrender, but even to aspire and strive for it is to join the company of the angels, and interject a few cracked notes into their triumphant choruses.

The disciples will have been in a quite different case. For them,

Jerusalem spelled danger, and perhaps disillusionment. There was every chance that Jesus would be arrested, and they be necessarily involved. He mystified them still. How could they be sure that it was not just the babbling of a disordered mind when he spoke of being one with the Father, a part of the very Godhead, with angels to watch over him; of the soon-to-come last days after which they would rule over the tribes of Israel on twelve thrones? If only, they said among themselves, he would show them a sign! Arrange for some dramatic manifestation of God's presence! That would settle the matter. But no sign was forthcoming. Or, rather, Jesus insisted that his teaching and his miraculous cures sufficed. They agreed that his teaching was inspiring and his miracles impressive, but in the menacing circumstances of their arrival in Jerusalem this was not enough. They wanted something they could see with their eyes and hear with their ears – like the Transfiguration about which, of course, they must have vaguely heard from the two disciples who were present. Now, as we read about them in the Gospels, their doubts and hesitations seem faint-hearted and even despicable; but at the time and in the circumstances they were understandable enough. How beautiful his sayings were! That he had brought light into the world so that none should dwell in darkness; that whoever loved his life would lose it and whoever hated his life in this world would keep it unto life eternal; that he had not come to judge the world but to save it. Beautiful sayings, yet to the disciples, mystifying, disturbing, bordering on the crazy. Coming from someone as poor and unlettered as they were themselves, someone who was jeered at and considered to be out of his mind by those they had been brought up to regard as their betters – like the Rabbis and Pharisees and Sadducees and Scribes, or Learned Counsel, as we should call them – how could they be sure that his sometimes wild and extravagant claims were well founded? Where, for instance, were the angels God was supposed to have provided to be his bodyguard? Where the clouds of glory he was to ride in on? Where the seraphim and cherubim who were to attend on him? Above all where were those twelve thrones? Thus I imagine them questioning themselves as Sancho Panza did when his Knight's fortunes seemed low, and the island Sancho was to reign over seemed tantalizingly remote.

And Judas? What was his attitude? Was he the most sceptical of them all about Jesus's Messianic pretensions and the powers that went therewith, and so the readier to be a paid renegade? Or was he the most understanding of them all, the one with the greatest certainty that Jesus was indeed all he claimed to be, Incarnate God, which made

Judas feel he must at all costs get rid of him? The method he chose
suggests as much – betraying Jesus to the Sanhedrin gang for a paltry
sum of money; thirty pieces of silver, which at the then market rate
was less than the cost of a mediocre slave. As does also the manner
he chose to identify Jesus – with a kiss. After all, there were plenty
of other means of identification than a kiss; such as pointing Jesus
out and pronouncing a Devil's version of *Ecce Homo* – Behold the

And as he went, they spread their clothes in the way.

DETAIL OF MOSAIC, PALERMO

Man! Surely the kiss was an indication that Judas betrayed Jesus, not because he hated him, but because he loved him. He could, and did, throw back the thirty pieces of silver at those who had paid them out to him, but the kiss could not be so easily disposed of. The kiss was for ever, and it was because he could not live with it that he killed himself. In *The Brothers Karamazov* Dostoevsky makes the returned Christ at the end of the Grand Inquisitor's tirade kiss him on his bloodless lips, whereupon the Inquisitor sends Christ away – 'Go, and come no more . . . come not at all, never, never . . .' – into the dark alleys of the town, but the kiss continues to glow in the Inquisitor's heart. Judas was the giver, not the recipient, of the kiss, and it was an icy chill, not a glow, that continued in his heart, becoming, finally, insupportable.

As the little company of Jesus and his disciples approached Jerusalem, two of the disciples were instructed to go ahead to a village that could be seen in the distance. There, they would find a she-ass tied up. The animal was to be unloosed and brought to Jesus. If anyone remonstrated, he was to be told that the Lord needed the ass, and all would be well. Everything happened, we are told, exactly as predicted; the ass was duly found, and its owner informed that it was needed, whereupon no difficulty was made about taking it away. It was on this ass that Jesus rode into Jerusalem, thereby fulfilling the words of the prophet Zechariah: *Thy King cometh unto thee . . . lowly, and riding upon an ass.*

According to the account in the Gospels, it was a truly triumphal entry. Enthusiastic onlookers tore off their garments and laid them on the ass by way of caparison, others *spread their garments upon the way*, or cut green branches from the trees to wave in the air or strew in Jesus's path. Some went before him and some followed, all crying: *Hosanna to the Son of David; Blessed is he that cometh in the name of the Lord; Hosanna in the highest.* As described, it was the sort of reception that a popular demagogue or national leader, a Gandhi or a Castro – for that matter, a Barabbas – might expect to be accorded. If it was indeed the case that Jesus not merely put up with being the hero of the occasion, but actually engineered it, then what happened was entirely out of keeping with all the rest of his ministry. Always before when anything of the kind threatened he was at great pains to discourage it, or, by disappearing, evaded it altogether. Obviously, the writers of the Gospels are aware of some difficulty here, and bring up the presence with Jesus of Lazarus – a subject of great public curiosity since he was raised from the dead – as an additional attraction. It is also implied that, momentarily, Jesus was popularly accepted as the long-waited Messiah, so that, more particularly as he was riding on an ass in accordance with the Scriptures, he could be sure just for this once of a rousing welcome on arriving in Jerusalem. Even so, Jesus riding on the ass was scarcely in keeping with the Jewish notion of how the Messiah would appear as a mighty king who would lay low the enemies and oppressors of the Children of Israel and then rule over the whole world.

May it not have been the case, then, that the cheers, and the spreading of clothes in Jesus's way, and the waving of palm branches, were, at any rate in some degree, ribald? Like the Roman soldiers attiring Jesus in a scarlet robe, and putting a crown of thorns on his head, and a reed in his right hand for a sceptre, and genuflecting before him with sham reverence. Or like the notice Pilate arranged to have put above Jesus's Cross, which so annoyed the chief priests: JESUS OF NAZARETH, THE KING OF THE JEWS. Ribaldry would seem to me to be more in keeping with the occasion, besides accounting for the total reversal of the crowd's mood so short a time later when they yelled for Jesus to be crucified. Also, for the fact that no word of Jesus had apparently been carried to Pilate prior to his actual appearance before him, whereas, as Governor of a notoriously turbulent Roman province, he would surely have heard about Jesus if his reception in Jerusalem had been as enthusiastic and regal as the Gospels suggest.

Jesus's whole ministry was directed against the pretensions of earthly power – the mundane equivalents of those Principalities and Powers which, St Paul said, cannot *separate us from the love of God*. The circumstances of his birth – whether mythical or actual, no matter; in fact, if mythical, the more significant in this connection – were calculated to establish his detachment from power and authority in human terms. How could a Messiah born in a manger, and so vulnerable before even as paltry a princeling as Herod that a flight into Egypt was necessary to evade his malign purposes, be regarded as the great king and warrior who would deliver God's Chosen People? Then the temptations in the wilderness, when the Devil made his offer of the kingdoms of the earth – claiming, with justice, that they were in his gift – which Jesus resolutely declined. When he was approached by someone important like Nicodemus, it never seems to have occurred to him, as it surely would to any ordinary evangelist or promoter of good causes, that such a man, with valuable contacts and influence, would be of service in his ministry. What he had to say to Nicodemus was precisely the same as what he had to say to the meanest beggar or the most disreputable tax-collector, the equivalent, then, of today's property-developer – that he must be reborn, and become a new man, a citizen thenceforth of Jesus's Kingdom which is not of this world. Again, in the case of the rich ruler, who wanted to know what he should do to inherit eternal life, Jesus made no suggestion that his wealth might be put to some good purpose – to endow a university, say, or institute a home for un-married mothers, or even to facilitate the propagation of Jesus's own teaching. All he was told to do was to dispose of his possessions to the poor; then, having become poor himself, and so blessed, he would be free to take up his cross and follow Jesus. I find it difficult to believe that some worthy Methodist nowadays, confronted by, say, the late Lord Rank in a similar mood, would have been likewise so general rather than particular in the advice he proffered.

In his teaching, too, Jesus continually stressed the fallacy of looking to this world and its rulers for help and guidance in fulfilling God's purposes; and though in the subsequent centuries his ostensible followers have often enough on his behalf gone after the support of the rich and the mighty, of millionaires and demagogues and kings and revolutionaries, or sought to become rich and mighty and fomentors of revolution themselves, the profound distrust of power which Jesus inculcated has lived on in the hearts of those who have loved him most and served him best. Caesar in all his different guises has continued to dazzle mankind, but the adulation a Caesar commands and requires, in the end curdles because a poor carpenter from Nazareth ironically insisted that Caesar's bills can be paid in Caesar's coinage, whereas what is due to God is everything we do and are and can be. This deflation of power would have seemed extra-ordinary to a Napoleon at the apogee of his career when he induced an obsequious Pope to place a crown on his Corsican head; to a Lenin transported from a sleazy Geneva *pension* to the Kremlin and the seat of the Tsar of All the Russias; or to a Hitler taking the salute as his goose-stepping contingents pounded down the Champs-Elysées. Yet such episodes prove to be written on water because an obscure Jew was crucified on the reluctant order of an insignificant Roman governor.

This theme runs through all the last phase of Jesus's life on earth. It is conveyed in the Passion and the events leading up to it and succeeding it, as a kind of sublime or celestial burlesque which Cervantes might have written when, at last, his stint in Purgatory served, he arrives in Heaven. Just as his hero, Don Quixote, follows out all the practices of chivalry, and enacts the adventures of the most illustrious knights, but with a flavour of grotesquerie, reflecting, not on him, but on them, so Jesus fulfils all the procedures of the prophecies, duly riding into Jerusalem on an ass to the plaudits of the multitude. Only, his victory lies in defeat, his glory in obscurity, his acclaim in ridicule. He is lifted up, truly, even *as Moses lifted up the serpent in the wilderness*, but on a Cross, to die in ignominy and agony. To the Rabbis and Pharisees this was a monstrous parody of a Messiah, and they took it for granted that Jesus was a charlatan. Their most merciful judgment was that he was mad – dangerously so. If, however, they had believed he was genuine, as some of them well may have done, they would have been even more enraged. Witness Judas, who, because he was convinced of the validity of Jesus's claims, betrayed him, instead of, like the other disciples, just running away.

The Italian Marxist, Passolini, in his film of the New Testament events, inevitably makes Jesus, on the occasion of his triumphal entry into Jerusalem, appear as a fiery and eloquent demagogue, in the style of a Garibaldi or a Lenin stirring up the mob to cast aside the chains of their servitude and inherit the earth. It is a stereotype that has become increasingly popular of late, but in the Gospels it finds little support. For one thing, at the great Jerusalem demo Jesus appears to have been totally silent and not to have responded in any way to the acclaim, whether genuine or ribald. Doubtless, his thoughts were far away – on the inexorable fulfilment of his destiny on earth, on the terrible ordeal that lay ahead, on those he was leaving behind and the heavy burden of responsibility that lay on their inadequate shoulders, on his return to his Father in Heaven to whom he taught his disciples to address their prayers, and through them, successive generations of Christians for twenty centuries.

What splendid opportunities for inflammatory oratory, all missed! At his trial, too, what a marvellous chance to confound and defy his accusers, thereby becoming a Dimitrov, a folk-hero, and incidentally providing invaluable material for future television commentaries. Jesus chose to be silent, alike before his accusers and his adulators, both when he was cheered and when he was reviled. When, earlier on, the mob had wanted to make him king, he hid; when they spat and jeered at him, he made no response; when they crucified him he prayed that they might be forgiven for they knew not what they did. He was Passolini's hero without the sound-track. The heroes and heroines of our time, more often than not, are portrayed in full oratorical spate, with their mouths furiously open and shutting and their arms furiously gesticulating. Jesus is a silent hero; if he is

My God, my God, why hast thou forsaken me?

DRAWING BY
GRAHAM SUTHERLAND

portrayed with his mouth open (as in Graham Sutherland's superb drawing), it is in groaning, not orating. He is the anti-demagogue, the lord of silence and of suffering.

It was at this time in the Temple that, according to the Gospels, Jesus chased out the hawkers and money-changers, rebuking them for making God's House, which Isaiah had said *shall be called an house of prayer*, into a *den of thieves*. Again, this action, like the triumphal entry into Jerusalem, can be taken as in the nature of a political demonstration, even though what concerned Jesus was the sanctity of the worship of God rather than economic exploitation or the independence of the Jewish State. In any case, he must have

145

known that they would be back the next day. They are there still. Watching Jesus beat them up, the disciples remembered the saying: *The zeal of thine house hath eaten me up.* Thus uplifted, and conscious that now he was having his last say before departing, Jesus went on teaching in the Temple in a way which, as we are told, held his listeners spell-bound. The impact was so strong that Jesus was asked for a sign to justify the high-handed action he had taken against the Temple traders, and the authority with which he had spoken afterwards. It was then that he delivered himself of an enigmatical remark which was to play an important part in his subsequent trial and conviction – *Destroy this temple and in three days I will raise it up.* His questioners were outraged; their magnificent Temple, built by Herod, called 'the Great', at enormous cost, had taken forty-six years to complete, and here was this crazy man from Nazareth, this nonentity without a penny to his name, claiming to be able to rebuild it in three days. It was preposterous.

In the Fourth Gospel it is explained that Jesus had in mind the temple of his body, which was to be crucified, and then in three days rise from the dead. What is more likely is that it was one of the wild exaggerations to which he was so humanly prone when he wanted to make a point – in this case, that his only authority, the only sign he could provide, was the intrinsic truth of what he had to say, compared with which the very Temple, whose sanctity he had been at such pains to uphold, was as transient and unsubstantial as all the other works of Time. In the same sort of vein, Jesus insisted that if an eye offends it should be plucked out, if an arm, it should be amputated; that we should forgive those who offend us, not just seven times, but seventy times seven, and that whoever calls his brother a fool risks hell fire. It is significant that pretty well the only charge against Jesus which could be made to stick was his remark about the Temple being destroyed and his being able to rebuild it in three days. As though Blake should have been executed for saying that a robin redbreast in a cage puts High Heaven in a rage, or that the strongest poison ever known comes from Caesar's laurel crown. As a result of the brilliance and fervour of Jesus's words on this occasion, the Fourth Gospel concludes, and still more of the miracles he performed, *many believed in his name.* None the less, he kept his head, not needing, or attaching much importance to, their testimony. *For he knew what was in man* – as, indeed, he did, none better.

As he left the Temple for the last time, Jesus told his disciples that it was doomed; *there shall not be left here one stone upon another, that shall not be thrown down.* He prophesied correctly; before forty years had passed the Temple had been razed to the ground, and it has never been rebuilt. Jesus's words, *that the Holy Place shall be left desolate for evermore* have been fulfilled, all that is left today being a fragment of wall for Rabbis to wail at. Otherwise, the Temple site is occupied by the Dome of the Rock, the Mosque of Omar, erected by the Moslems in AD 688. On the Mount of Olives the disciples gathered round Jesus and pressed him to tell them when exactly the catastrophes he predicted might be expected. This, he told them, was God's secret, but there would be signs and portents. False prophets would arise; wars, plagues, famines, earthquakes and other disasters might be expected. Chaos and destruction would befall the world, and for many the only recourse would be flight, which they would have to undertake at the shortest notice, making off and leaving their homes and even their families behind them. Perhaps worst of all, conflict and strife would afflict the human race, brother turning against brother, and father against son. So Jesus built up his picture of the Apocalypse and the coming of the last days, after which *the Son of man shall come in his glory, and all the angels with him, then shall he sit upon the throne of his glory : And before him shall be gathered all nations; and he shall separate them one from another, as the shepherd divideth his sheep from the goats.*

The disciples will have listened in trepidation. How could they be sure that they would be ready when zero hour came? Or that they would be truly numbered with the sheep, and not suffer the fate of the goats and be told: *Depart from me, ye cursed, into everlasting fire, prepared for the devil and his angels?* Through the subsequent centuries Christians have gone on looking at the world's happenings for signs that Jesus's predictions were about to come true, and have rarely looked in vain. The disasters which were to presage his Second Coming have proved to be endemic, and never more so than in the twentieth century. As I write these words apocalyptic intimations are multiplying, to the point that many see the last days as soon to be upon us. For believers, Christianity has thus been a condition of continuing alertness. No state of mind could be more appropriate to our human condition, enabling us, as it does, to see each day as perhaps marking the end of Time – as each issue of a newspaper must have a lead story of olympian significance, and then, once published, fades away to nothingness, useful only to light fires and wrap fish, while another issue with another lead story of olympian significance comes off the presses.

So Jesus told his disciples that only God knew when the world would end, but that they must live in perpetual readiness for its ending, watching for the signs – the false prophets, the earthquakes, the plagues, the wars – and, like the wise virgins awaiting the bridegroom, be ever ready for his coming. The signs are always in evidence; there is no lack ever of false prophets (in our time, a record batch!), or of wars and upheavals and pestilences. The world is always ending, Jesus is always coming, and we are forever in transit – on our way to a destination which, like Augustine's City of God, is beyond our reach but within our comprehension. As for being judged at the great divide, when the Son of Man comes in his glory with all the angels in attendance, to take his seat upon his throne and separate the sheep from the goats – no great law books will be required for reference, no Learned Counsel to gather their gowns round them and expound and dispute, no witnesses to be called and cross-examined. Simply, Jesus will claim as his own those who, when he was hungry and thirsty and homeless and naked, had succoured him. If, incredulously, they say they have no memory of performing these services, it will be explained to them that in performing them for others they performed them for him. Contrariwise, those who failed to minister to the needs of others will be seen as thereby failing to minister to Jesus's needs, and so fit only to be expelled from his presence and cast into outer darkness. Such will be the simple test. And who dare face it?

Jesus had come to Jerusalem to celebrate the Feast of the Passover with his disciples. Though he quarrelled with ultra-orthodox Jews over their legalistic attitude to the Mosaic Code – as when they insisted that healing someone, or even idly plucking ears of corn, on the Sabbath was sinful – he scrupulously followed the normal Jewish observances. It is true that helping his neighbour – which, as he showed in the parable of the Good Samaritan, meant everyone in need of help – making himself available to them, whoever they might be, rich or poor, respectable or of dubious repute, always took precedence over the minutiae of ritual, such as the rules for ablution before eating; but in essentials he observed the precepts and practices of orthodox Judaism. Otherwise, we may be sure, his enemies would have accused him, not just of occasional laxity, but of lapsing altogether from the religion of his fathers, to which, as a Jew, he inalienably belonged.

This was to be, he knew, his last Passover; the last occasion on which, as a mortal man, he would participate in an act of worship and thankfulness with his disciples, who were, after all, very dear to him. The Passover itself symbolized a release – of the Children of Israel from Egypt; it, too, was supposed to be celebrated in a state of readiness to depart, just as he had told the disciples to live in readiness

for his return, with all their earthly ties and commitments wound up, so that they could depart at a moment's notice. Thus, the old Jewish feast was entirely appropriate for the new Christian feast; the one became the other, comprehending both.

In the story of Jesus this celebration of what came to be called the Last Supper, in which the old Passover is transmuted into the new Eucharist, is one of the great climaxes, along with the Nativity, the Baptism, the Crucifixion and the Resurrection, and as such has been portrayed in innumerable ways through the centuries of Christendom, in words and music and paint and marble and stone – in every representational medium known or devised. According to the Gospels' account, the celebration took place in an upper room put at Jesus's disposition for the purpose in the same sort of way as was the ass on which he rode into Jerusalem. Peter and John were instructed –

149

it is perhaps significant that it was they, rather than Judas, who would normally be in charge of such arrangements – to go into Jerusalem, and when they saw a man carrying a pitcher of water they were to follow him into the house he was making for. There they were to say to the goodman of the house: *Where is the guest chamber where I shall eat the passover with my disciples?* They would thereupon be shown a larger furnished upper room, in which they were to make all necessary preparations. It is usually suggested that in the case both of the ass and the upper room, the donors were people with whom Jesus had quasi-clandestine contacts. Though the matter is of little importance, it would seem to me that in the drama of Jesus's last days and hours the circumstances for it shaped themselves; so powerful a script, as it were, producing its own props and extras. In the same sort of way, a sleep-walker never stumbles or falters; the skull is ready to Hamlet's hand, Socrates does not need to call for his hemlock, nor the serpent in the Garden of Eden to hunt for an apple.

The traditional scene is a long table with Jesus in the middle and the disciples ranged on either side of him, with John, described as the disciple he loved, next to him. In the Roman style, they recline on couches. Probably, it was something a good deal more primitive; they were poor men with simple ways, especially the fishermen, whose like are to be seen today in Asia Minor eating their meals – a hunk of bread and a newly caught fish; the selfsame food distributed to the five thousand – amidst their nets and boats. Jesus tells the disciples of his great desire to have this Passover with them, knowing that *his hour was come that he should depart out of this world unto the Father, having loved his own which were in the world, he loved them unto the end.* They still only vaguely understand what he is getting at. He has one last practical lesson for them, and to demonstrate it, takes off his outer garments, puts a towel round himself, and goes from one to the other – including Judas – to wash their feet; first wetting them, and then wiping them with the towel. This done, he puts on his clothes again, resumes his place at the table, and explains the significance of his action. They call him Master, and rightly so, but in washing their feet the Master deliberately abases himself in order to demonstrate that greatness lies, not in self-assertion, but in self-abnegation. Earthly authority displays itself in giving orders, in magnificent apparel, in hordes of servitors, in sycophantic addresses; the authority Jesus disposes of is, by contrast, spiritual, and expresses itself in serving, not being served, in seeking to be the least instead of the greatest, the last instead of the first, in finding wisdom in the innocence of children and truth in the foolishness of men rather than

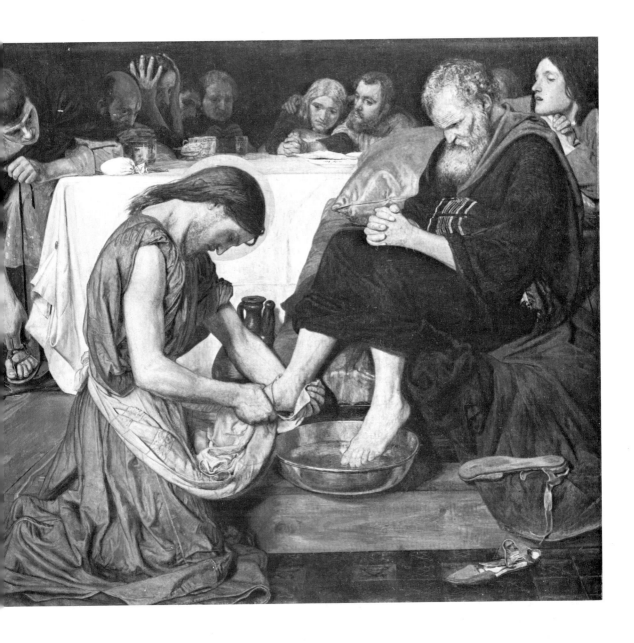

He began to wash the disciples' feet, and to wipe them with the towel wherewith he was girded.

PAINTING BY FORD
MADOX BROWN

in those who pass for being sagacious and experienced in the world's ways. When we want to adulate men, we say they are godlike; but when God became Man, it was in the lineaments of the least of men.

In washing the disciples' feet Jesus demonstrated once and for all that the Son of Man was the servant of men; that whatsoever was arrogant, assertive, dogmatic or demogogic belonged to the gospel of power, not to his gospel of love; that humility is not just virtuous but the very condition of all virtue, and that in abasing themselves, men

151

attain the highest heights, as, in glorifying themselves, they sink to the lowest depths. One of Jesus's greatest gifts was to release a tidal wave of humility, flowing through the world against the Devil's contrary tide of self-assertion – the Devil being the great I Am, and Jesus the great We Are. Thanks to this, the laughter of the saints has drowned the trumpets of the great; the nakedness of the saints mocked the splendour of captains and kings; the foolishness of the saints confuted the wit and wisdom of the learned. Every court has its Fool, and the Fool is Jesus. If the greatest of all, Incarnate God, chooses to be the servant of all, who will wish to be the master? If he receives orders, who will venture to give them? If those who climb are descending, and those who descend, climbing, who will aspire after eminence? These are the questions Jesus leaves with us; not to answer – because they have no answer – but to live with and by. Christianity is a stupendous riddle without a solution; a stupendous joke without a point; a stupendous song without a tune; a stupendous waking dream that we lose in sleeping; a death in life and a life in death.

The Passover begins with breaking bread; something that in itself is very beautiful at all times as signifying the sharing of food, our body's first necessity, with one another. When bread is broken, it is made available; and, in a company, each taking a piece unites them as, before being broken, the bread was united. So, its breaking is an assurance that the participants are brothers and cannot harm one another. This is the most ancient of all sacraments. Jesus, however, on the occasion of his last Passover, went further, and when he had broken the bread and given it to his disciples – still including Judas – he added the mysterious words: *This is my body which is given for you : this do in remembrance of me.* In like manner he took the cup, saying *This . . . is the new testament in my blood, which is shed for you.* He had spoken in this sort of strain before. For instance, when he told the woman of Samaria that he could give her living water, and that, after drinking it, she would never thirst again. It was water that would become, for whoever drank it, a *well . . . springing up into everlasting life.* Or when in Galilee he spoke of being the *bread of life.* This was not, he said, like the manna in the wilderness, which the Children of Israel ate, but which did not prevent them from dying. It was living bread, which also *came down from Heaven* and *if any man eat of this bread, he shall live for ever : and the bread that I will give is my flesh, which I will give for the life of the world.* Later, in the synagogue in Capernaum, according to the Fourth Gospel, he was even more explicit: *Except ye eat the flesh of the Son of man, and drink his blood, ye have no life in you. . . . For my flesh is meat indeed, and my blood is drink indeed. He that eateth my flesh, and drinketh my blood, dwelleth in me, and I in him. As the living Father hath sent me, and I live by the Father: so he that eateth me, even he shall live by me.*

At the Last Supper this notion of Jesus's flesh and blood becoming, not just, like manna, sustenance now, the food of Time, but everlasting sustenance, food for Eternity – this mysterious notion was made actual. His flesh was veritably handed out in morsels of bread, his blood in a cup of wine. The twelve, Judas included, ate him and drank him, in a celebration which was to provide the early Church with its basic act of worship; already being practised in the time of the Apostle Paul, and continuing in one form or another to the present day, so that through the past twenty centuries there has certainly never been a week, maybe never a day or an hour even, when someone somewhere was not dispensing the body and blood of Jesus, or at any rate recalling that Last Supper in Jerusalem and Jesus's words at it by munching a morsel of bread and swallowing a sip of wine. So many variations in procedure, but always the same essential theme of a man offering his physical existence, his flesh and blood, in order that other men might know and experience a spiritual existence which was everlasting. Thus, a Pope in majestic vestments intones the words – *Take, eat; this is my body. . . . Drink ye all of* [*this*]; *for this is my blood* – at his High Altar in St Peter's, its cavernous space overflowing with accompanying music which expresses the same mystical joy in the sacrifice of Calvary, in the Lamb of God that takes away the sins of the world. Thus, too, in his own austere style, a stern Presbyterian minister in a black gown with stony reverence offers bread and unfermented wine to his flock in remembrance of that gathering in Jerusalem when Jesus made his final dispositions before submitting himself to the laws of men and the Cross. Innumerable variations in the commemoration, but always the same event and the same words recalled.

The worshippers wait at the altar rails, like famished dossers at a soup-kitchen, their mouths open, their hands outspread; then return to their places visibly revived. '*Hereux les invités au repas du Seigneur! Voici l'Agneau de Dieu qui enlève le péché du monde*', the priest says in the French Mass as he dispenses the consecrated bread, *Le Corps du Christ*. Happy, indeed, the guests at this feast, but I, alas, have never been among them, nor most probably ever will be. Sadly, I have to admit that its sublime symbolism has always eluded me. The magic of transubstantiation fails to work; the wafer and the wine fall on my tongue as wafer and wine, and are swallowed, if at all, as such. For me, only the Fearful Symmetry of life itself has seemed truly convincing; all secondary versions or simulations – such as a monarch elaborately anointed to be a symbolic Head of State, a military tattoo to convey a battle, porn for passion or celluloid for flesh – are ultimately untenable. Similarly, with the bread-flesh and the wine-blood. Was this, I ask myself, what sent Judas out into the night to betray his Master? – that the bread and wine remained for him, as for me, untransubstantiated, the Presence unreal?

Jesus, of course, knows that Judas will betray him, even though he has washed his feet along with the others, and given him, too, his flesh to eat and his blood to drink. It would have been perfectly easy for him to denounce Judas there and then; to shame him into admitting his evil intention, and perhaps even induce him to abandon it, or at least to change his plan, thereby sparing himself that terrible kiss. Yet he desists, contenting himself with just announcing that one of them will betray him. But which one? He half tells them, but, as so often, they fail to grasp his meaning. Maybe they were not intended to, and the secret had to be kept; maybe they did not want to know, or even feared to know. When Judas gets up to leave, Jesus says to him: *That thou doest, do quickly*. The others suppose that Jesus is sending him out to buy things they need, or to distribute alms to the poor, as was customary at Passover time. Judas, the Fourth Gospel tells us, *went immediately out and it was night* – another unforgettable compression of meaning into seven words.

Jesus never once reproaches Judas; neither before nor after the betrayal. He, after all, has a role in the drama in which they are both involved as inexorable in its own way as Jesus's; a cup of bitterness to drink from which he, too, might have wished to be delivered. Understanding, as Jesus did, the deepest springs of human conduct, he must have pitied Judas; a forlorn and tragic figure. Or so he seemed to me as I sat thinking about him, at what purports to be the scene of his ultimate suicide, called the Field of Blood, where, *falling headlong, he burst assunder in the midst, and all his bowels gushed out*. The site is probably even more dubious than most of the Holy Land ones; as are doubtless the details given in the Acts of the Apostles of Judas's end. Yet still the place seemed benighted and accursed; I dare say, in consequence of the many hundreds of thousands of visitors who over the years had seen it so. Then, suddenly, it occurred to me that, since Jesus made no exceptions in the beneficiaries under his death, since he died for all men, he might be said to have died even for Judas. The thought so delighted me that I kept on repeating to myself: *Jesus died even for Judas!* as though I had made some extraordinary discovery. Perhaps in a way I had.

After Judas's departure, and the mysterious circumstances accompanying it, Jesus obviously feels he must reassure the remaining eleven. Even now they cannot understand – and who shall blame them? – why, being under God's special protection, with angels for guardians, Jesus must still succumb to the machinations of an insignificant body like the Sanhedrin. How he can, at one and the same time, claim to be part of the Godhead, and yet appear so utterly defenceless; set himself up as the Messiah, and in the same breath speak of being a sacrificial lamb. Where he is going, he tells them, they cannot come, though later they will be able to follow him. But where *is* he going? And *why* can't they follow him now? It is Peter, of course, who blurts out that, whatever Jesus may say, he, Peter, will straightway follow him where he is going, to the point of laying down his life for him. Jesus picks him up in his old ironical manner – 'You'll lay down your life for me? Will you now? Well, I'll tell you something . . .' and there follows that heart-rending prediction about how Peter the very next morning will deny him thrice before the cock crows.

Jesus knows them, has no illusions about them. After all, they are but men; they will run away, they will quarrel, they will alter his words and distort his teaching. Thus reflecting, I imagine him looking at them with particular tenderness. How preposterous they are! How unworthy, how foolish, how dear! Prototypes of all the great army of his followers to come; the popes, the archbishops and bishops, the evangelists, the revivalists, the saints and the charlatans, the theologians and the speakers with tongues and the friars and the hermits, the crusaders and the very parfait knights and the hot-gospellers; yes, and the scribblers hoping belatedly to lay a few hesitant words at his feet to compensate for all the others blown away like dust. Ah, what he is unloosing on the world! If only, even now, while he is still with them in the flesh, they would heed one new last commandment that he has for them – *that ye love one another; as I have loved you, that ye also love one another*. Then all would be well with them; then they need have no worries; then everyone would know *that ye are my disciples, if ye have love one to another*.

It must have been a moment of great exaltation; Jesus, his eyes shining, his face radiant as at the Transfiguration, and the others, sharing his mood, momentarily caught up in their oneness with him and with one another. Yet how utterly characteristic of human beings, then and always, that even with Jesus's sublime words freshly in their ears, the disciples begin to contend together as to which of them is to be accounted the greatest in Heaven! It was a preposterous lapse from grace on the disciples' part, when they had just had the unique privilege of hearing from Jesus's own lips the call to wear as a badge of discipleship their love for him and for one another. So preposterous a lapse that it must have been a temptation to the writers of the Gospels to leave the episode out. It had to go in, though. Without such lapses, how should we ever acquire the humility to grasp our own imperfection, and so conceive and aspire after perfection? How, for that matter, should we ever laugh – laughter being born of an awareness of the gap between what we are and what we aspire to be, between the perfection we can conceive and the intrinsic imperfection of all our works. And the wider the gap the louder the laugh. If we could love selflessly for ever, put aside once and for all cupidity, lechery, vanity and all the other black demons of the will, why then the soap-opera of our mortal existence would have to come to an end for lack of any comic relief. The Fall of Man would be rescinded, the Garden of Eden become a garden city, and the knowledge of Good and Evil which brought about the expulsion of Adam and Eve from paradise, disappear along with Good and Evil themselves. There would be no art, no literature, no music; only television documentaries on Civilization, the Ascent of Man, and other such themes. Unceasing journeying on a celestial motorway, interminably rising heavenwards and descending hellwards on moving stairways.

According to the Fourth Gospel, at this point Jesus proceeded to give the disciples an account, at once realistic and resassuring, of how they might expect to fare in the world when he was no longer with them in his bodily existence. They were not to worry, he told them; *in my Father's house are many mansions: if it were not so, I would have told you*, and they might be confident that he would go ahead to prepare a place for them. Thomas, the doubter, asked, not unreasonably, how, if they did not know where Jesus was going, they could possibly be expected to follow after him. It was then that Jesus came out with one of his greatest sayings – that he was himself *the way, the truth, and the life*. For his followers, to know him is to know where they are going, and why they are going there, and to be vouchsafed the strength to follow the way to the end, where Jesus awaits them. There are many signposts, but he is the way! there are many words and meanings, but he is the truth; there are many ways of living and dying, but he is life itself. For an illustration he turned to the vineyards all around them, at that season still in leaf and already pruned, with branches strewn about the ground; some of them green, and some dried in the sun and ready to be burned. *I am the true vine*, Jesus said: God the Father is the husbandman, and the disciples are the branches, which, if they bear fruit, become part of the life of the vine; if not, they are pruned away to wither and be cast on the fire. In the world, the disciples must expect to be hated, as he has been hated; *if ye were of the world, the world would love his own: but because ye are not of the world, but I have chosen you out of the world, therefore the world hateth you.* Lest they lose heart and become fearful, he goes on, a Comforter will come to them to strengthen and sustain them. This is the Holy Ghost or Holy Spirit, the Third Person of the Trinity, thereby completing the whole human conspectus, with God the Father creator of the universe, God the Son who dwelt and dwells among us, full of grace and truth, and God the Holy Ghost, to be our Comforter.

How strange, to a twentieth-century mind, to find that this ancient, creaking notion of the Trinity, recalling, as it does, bored scholastics poring stoically over forgotten tomes from their monastery library, still works perfectly; rather as though in an energy crisis some old abandoned water-wheel were to be reactivated, turning cheerfully and efficiently, and worthily grinding corn as of yore. First, God the Father, who is everywhere and nowhere; the Oneness of all things rather than any particular thing. Thus Augustine, in a remarkable passage in the *Confessions*, asks himself what he loves when he loves his God. Is it material or temporal beauty? Surely not. Not the brilliance of earthly light, the sweet melody of harmony and song, the fragrance of flowers, and perfumes; not manna or honey or limbs such as the body delights to embrace. It is none of these he loves when he loves his God. Yet, in loving God, he also loves them; but in his inner self, when his soul is bathed in illimitable light, when it breathes fragrance not borne away on the wind, listens to sounds that never die away, clings to an embrace not severed by desire's fulfilment. What, then, is his God? He asks the earth, and it answers: I am not God. Likewise he asks the sea, the winds that blow, the sky, the sun, the moon and the stars, all things that can be admitted by the door of the senses, and the answer of one and all is the same – they are not God. Where, then is God? And the answer is, at the very core of creation, and in all its parts. God is creation's soul, and because we have souls which are components of His as the tiniest particle of moisture in sea spray is a component of the ocean, we are one with God, as God is one with us. So Augustine triumphantly concludes: 'He is the life of the life of my soul.'

God the Father is both far away and near at hand; His voice is, at once, deafening in its thunderousness, and too still and small to be easily audible. In our Earthly City we can receive signals from the Heavenly City where God resides, and, equally, transmit signals to Him there, but a deep, impassable chasm divides the two Cities. To cross this chasm, we need a suspension-bridge, which, seemingly so frail, rocking in the wind, yet, for those with the courage and the faith to traverse it, provides a passage. This suspension-bridge is God the Son. Through him we may know God truly as a Father; through him, the universal becomes the particular, the immanent becomes the transcendent, the implicit becomes the explicit, Always becomes Now. The pure of heart, Jesus tells us, are blessed because they may know God the Father; but thanks to God the Son, so may the impure of heart through knowing Jesus. It was for this purpose – to open up a way for sinners to know God – that Jesus came among us. By the same token, this was the offence for which he was crucified. God the Son is God the Father's probation officer to a fallen world, who, by his death on the Cross, expiated Adam's sin, and reversed the Fall. Under the dispensation of God the Father, Adam brought death into the world; under the dispensation of God the Son, Jesus abolished death.

Then there is the Holy Ghost, described by Jesus as the *Comforter . . . even, the Spirit of truth; whom the world cannot receive*, but who will stay with the disciples for ever and teach them all things. Of the three elements in the Trinity, this is in conception the most nebulous, but in terms of experience, the most actual. It first descended upon the disciples, we are told in the Acts of the Apostles, on the first Pentecost, fifty days after Passover, on what is celebrated by Christians as Whit Sunday; manifesting itself in *a sound . . . as of a rushing mighty wind*, while the disciples seemed to be on fire, and so filled with the Holy Spirit that they *began to speak with other tongues as the Spirit gave them utterance*. Whatever may have been the precise intimations and nature of the experience, it is certainly the case that thenceforth these hitherto easily scared, rather quarrelsome and confused men became worthy and effective servants of their Master; propagandists of genius and martyrs of indomitable heroism, as is attested by the manner in which the early Church, whose first members they were, spread and throve. Moreover, it is also an indisputable fact that since their time there have been innumerable testimonies of a similar experience and transformation wrought by the working of the Holy Spirit. Indeed, there must be very few who have seriously tried to become followers of Jesus without in some degree going through this experience. It is as though, on a cold grey day, suddenly the sun comes out and suffuses the whole of one's being with its heat and light. Words break from lips not normally particularly eloquent, or are traced by a pen outside the volition of its holder. They come pouring forth, unconstrained in the strait-jacket of meaning, reaching after some other, higher synthesis. Other faces

cannot be strangers because, with all men and women brothers and sisters, there are no strangers. Discord has gone, leaving only harmony; conflict has gone, leaving only peace; hatred has gone, leaving only love. All is orderly, serene, joyous. St John of the Cross tells us of the dark night of the soul; this is its bright day.

Jesus explains to the disciples how desperately they are going to need the Holy Spirit. Because they have seen and walked with reality, the world, which loves fantasy, will hate them as it has hated Jesus himself; because they speak truth, the world, which loves lies, will persecute them as it has persecuted Jesus. When they lose heart, as they surely will, the Comforter will be there to restore their courage; as, when they, too, get involved in fantasy, it will be there to draw them back to reality, and, when words fail them, to unseal their lips. I have often, myself, sat in darkness, and cried aloud for the Holy Spirit to deliver me from the fantasies that gather round a parched soul like flies round a rotting carcass in the desert. Likewise, sat tongue-tied, crying out to be given utterance, and delivered from the apprehensions which afflict the earth-bound. And never, ultimately, in vain. Jesus's promise is valid; the Comforter needs only to be summoned. The need is the call, the call is the presence, and the presence is the Comforter, the Spirit of Truth.

Now, in the Garden of Gethsemane where Jesus has repaired with his disciples – less Judas, of course – a terrible sadness descends upon him. The remaining part of the drama of his earthly life must be played alone; he has only God for company, and at times loses contact even with Him. *Sit ye here, while I go and pray yonder*, he tells the disciples, and, detaching three of them – Peter, James and John – from the others to accompany him, he makes for the quietest part of the Garden. *My soul*, he confides to them, *is exceeding sorrowful, even unto death*. Was it, perhaps, a temptation to Jesus to take his own life in order to evade the terrible ordeal that lay ahead? Not just the arrest, the ignominy, the harassment, the trial and execution with all its grisly accompaniments; rather, the sense of failure, hearing his own exalted words used in jeering mockery, wondering himself whether, after all, his ministry has been a piece of fantasy, his Kingdom and his life guttering out together. If, in Jesus's despair, any such intention was entertained, it can have been only momentarily; he knew beyond any shadow of doubt what was required of him, and that God would give him strength and faith and serenity to go through with it. His present need is to draw near to God; let the three disciples then, *tarry . . . and watch with me*, while he withdraws to about a stone's throw away. There, he falls upon his knees, his head bowed down so low that it touches the ground, and prays his anguished prayer: *O my Father, if it be possible, let this cup pass from me.*

Jesus had previously told the disciples that whatever was prayed for sincerely in his name would be granted, to the point that mountains could be made to move themselves by prayer. If, therefore, he had truly asked God to deliver him from betrayal by Judas and all its consequences, his prayer would surely have been answered, and he have been spared the agony and bloody sweat that lay ahead. But, of course, there was the proviso; it must be, not as he willed, but as God willed. And it was God's will that he should be nailed to a cross, and thereby, as the victim of this, perhaps the cruellest form of execution ever devised, provide mankind for ever after with a fount of joy and hope, an inspiration to high endeavour, and a certainty of salvation.

How long he stayed with his forehead pressed to the ground while the answer to his prayer made its way into his consciousness, is not clear, but it was long enough for Peter and James and John to be all three snoring when he returns to them. They could not, he ruefully reflects, manage to keep awake even for one hour; thus indulging himself for once, most humanly, in a mood of self-pity. Then he stirs them up, not too gently I should surmise, telling them: *Watch ye and pray, lest ye enter into temptation,* adding a much-quoted phrase which is almost a definition of our human condition: *The spirit indeed is willing, but the flesh is weak.* After all their brave words they had proved unable to carry out the little duty he had entrusted to them – just to keep watch, presumably with a view to alerting him if Judas and the Sanhedrin's men turned up. He would not wish to be discovered by them in a posture of supplication. Poor fellows! Their eyes are heavy, and when Jesus resumes his prayers they again drop off. This time it seems that Jesus's agony is so terrible that, according to St Luke's Gospel, *his sweat was as it were great drops of blood falling down to the ground.*

What went on inside Jesus, what fears and hopes alternated to produce the extreme fluctuations in his state of mind between a joyous acceptance of God's will and a desperate cry to be delivered from the supreme sacrifice required of him, we cannot know and scarcely dare speculate. Thenceforth, words and thought processes become an irrelevance. As in great grief or great ecstasy, silence reigns, and any word – the most loving, eloquent, perceptive, meaningful, understanding – falls like a dead stone into a still pond. On the one hand, a man called on to suffer beyond the limits that flesh can be expected to endure; on the other, God himself on the rack over

Father, if thou be willing,
remove this cup from me :
nevertheless not my will,
but thine, be done.

PAINTING BY EL GRECO

the inadequacy of the creation to which He had accorded free will –
as a Shakespeare might beat his breast over the paltriness of Lear's
rage, or a Bach groan over the pedestrian notes of his *St Matthew
Passion*, or an El Greco despairingly avert his eyes from his lustreless
portraiture. This is the beginning of what is called the 'Passion' – a
mysterious word signifying, at one and the same time, the greatest
imaginable suffering and the greatest imaginable absorption in
another person; affliction carried to the point when it becomes
ecstatic, and two bodies, minds and souls made molten, and dis-
solving into each other to become one:

> But as all several souls contain
> Mixture of things they know not what,
> Love these mix'd souls doth mix again,
> And makes both one, each this, and that.

Jesus's Passion, in the very intensity of its suffering, cauterized all
suffering, so that at the highest attainable point in the experience of
living, when a man stands at the very extremity of his mortality,
teetering on its brink, as it were, he can vaguely become aware that
affliction itself is a manifestation of God's mercy and love, and offer
his affliction to God as a rare and precious sacrifice. Equally, the love
that overflowed from Jesus's Passion, like the blood from his wounds,
makes us all one, with him and with one another, as human lovers are
made one by their human passion.

Jesus himself said that the greatest act of disinterestedness a human
being was capable of was to lay down his life for his friends. He,
however, was not to have the consolation of dying for someone; he
had to die for everyone. Thus to die for mankind is, in human terms,
an abstraction; like being the Unknown Warrior in Westminster
Abbey, or under the Arc de Triomphe, rather than the hero awarded
a posthumous Victoria Cross. Sacrifice, like love, has to be a two-way
affair to be humanly satisfying; there is a Who Whom? in it as there
is in revolution. Jesus's sacrifice had so immense an orbit that it must
have seemed to him as though the circuit might never be completed.
We who know the stupendous consequences of what he did, think of
him as sustained by the certainty of the sublime outcome; the lonely
man in the Garden of Gethsemane whose little band of nondescript
followers cannot be relied on even to keep awake at his behest, and will
soon anyway scatter, has only his special relationship with God, and
his inner certainty of the validity of the mission entrusted to him, to
buoy him up when he confronts the prospect of falling into the hands
of enemies resolved to kill him.

The only possible explanations of Jesus's state of mind at this time are, either that he was completely mad, and possessed of a megalomaniac death-wish; or that he was a crazy charlatan caught in the toils of his own deceptions; or that, as the Gospels say, he was veritably Incarnate God, and had to die in accordance with the prophecies in order that thenceforth men might be reborn into a new spiritual existence, experiencing on earth God's everlasting kingdom of love, whence they had come and whither they were going. If Jesus was deluded, then his delusions have provided the truth for countless millions of Christians, from the most simple to the most sophisticated; if he was mad, then his madness has been Christendom's sanity for two thousand years; if he was, as he claimed, in a special and particular sense the Son of God, then the words spoken and the deeds done, the death died and the life resurrected, make a whole, and that whole our salvation. *And there are also many other things which Jesus did*, the Fourth Gospel concludes, *the which, if they should be written every one, I suppose that even the world itself could not contain the books that should be written* – a sentence, incidentally, very touching and sympathetic to vendors of words (as St Augustine calls us) who are prone to resort to such observations when we have filled our space without exhausting our subject. Since that time, many, many books about what Jesus did have veritably been written, though the world still manages to contain them – just – and many more no doubt will be written; but taken together, they are only like the basketsful gathered up after the five thousand had been fed. The basic provender, the five barley loaves and two fishes, are, and ever will remain, the Gospels themselves.

Returning once more to the disciples, and finding them yet again asleep, this time Jesus tells them to *sleep on now, and take your rest*. It just does not matter any more whether they are awake or asleep. For the time being, they are irrelevant. The hour of Jesus's betrayal has come: *he that betrayeth me is at hand*. Now there arrives on the scene a crowd, led by Judas, of Roman legionaries and Temple guards, as well as miscellaneous hangers-on of the kind drawn to stare at a street accident or at someone preparing to commit suicide by jumping off a high building. The legionaries and guards are armed with swords and staves, and some are carrying lanterns or torches. A lurid scene. All action is melodramatic; exciting rather than interesting, theatre rather than life. Jesus's solitude is over; the world has intruded into the Garden of Gethsemane, and he is about to be delivered *into the hands of sinners*. The arrangement is that when Judas kisses Jesus it will be the signal for him to be taken into custody – but carefully, because of his supernatural powers. How typical of the worldly to suppose that powers which will heal the sick and restore sanity to the deranged can equally be used to fight off a physical attack! As though the skill of a manipulative surgeon would be similarly effective in breaking, as in mending, bones. Judas is hesitant; he keeps putting off the fateful moment – the kiss that can never be undone. So Jesus himself steps forward and asks whom they are seeking. *Jesus of Nazareth*, they say, and he replies, laconically: *I am he*. Then, according to the Fourth Gospel, a very strange thing happens; Judas and the others all fall back, and with one accord bow down before Jesus.

The power of truth is very great, as even those who, preferring fantasy, hate it and seek to destroy it, are in the last resort forced to acknowledge. Their sense of its power is manifested by their very proneness to shout it down and stamp it out. Thus, the men stoning Stephen had to stop their ears and rush furiously upon him, having been cut to the heart by his shining words and face; and even wicked old Karamazov found himself on his knees in the presence of Father Zossima, although he had come there to ridicule him. Similarly, it was a reflex action on the part of the rabble who had come with Judas to take Jesus, to abase themselves before him. Recovering, they resume their menacing posture, and Jesus again asks them: *Whom seek ye?*, to be given the same response: *Jesus of Nazareth*. Again, he replies: *I am he*, adding this time that they are free to take him. He only asks that *these* – pointing to the disciples – may be allowed *to go their way*. With the exception of Peter and John, the disciples now disappear from the story until the Resurrection and the coming of the Holy Ghost to strengthen and inspire them.

Still there is no move to apprehend Jesus; the agreed signal – Judas's kiss – is awaited. It is, for Judas, the final humiliation that his betrayal of Jesus is, as it turns out, unnecessary; the kiss purposeless. Yet still it cannot be evaded; each man his own torturer and executioner. He steps forward – *forthwith he came to Jesus, and saith, Hail master; and kissed him*. Still there is no reproach. *Friend*, Jesus says mildly, *wherefore art thou come?* I try to imagine, vainly, the despair that must now have engulfed Judas – what he has lost, what he has done, and all to no end. How he rushes away from the scene, the others, having no more use for him and indifferent whether he stays or goes, glad not to have any further occasion to remember his existence. How then, full of remorse, he takes back the thirty pieces of silver to the chief priests and elders, who refuse to receive them – *what is that to us? See thou to that*. Whereupon, he throws the money

down in the sanctuary, and goes away and kills himself. What else was there for him to do?

This is the first occasion on which Jesus finds himself confronted with power in its naked shape of violence. He has been, of course, aware of Roman imperial might – the soldiery, the weapons, the pomp and circumstance. If he had accepted the Devil's offer of the Kingdoms of the earth, he would have been at the dispensing, not receiving, end of authority; a giver of orders rather than their victim, part of the power *apparat*. As it is, he finds himself *reckoned among the transgressors*. Previously, he had told the disciples that in such an eventuality, contrary to his instructions on sending them off on their missionary journeys, when they were to take nothing with them, this time *he that hath a purse, let him take it, and likewise his scrip, and he that hath no sword, let him sell his garment and buy one.* Taking him at his literal word, the disciples produced two swords with which they had provided themselves. It was, presumably, one of these swords that Peter had brought with him into the Garden of Gethsemane. When he sees Jesus apprehended by the legionaries and Temple guards and hemmed in by the rabble, he draws the sword and attacks one of the High Priest's servants – a man named Malchus – cutting off his ear. Jesus at once heals the wound, and makes another of those sublime pronouncements which were to ring through the world for centuries to come. Telling Peter to put up his sword, he adds: *For all they that take the sword, shall perish with the sword.*

It is a saying that has proved to be true in all circumstances and at all levels of violence; from the squalid little terrorist who lurks under cover to aim his shot when the occasion offers, to the great campaigns and battlefields of history. Victor and vanquished alike exemplify the saying; having resorted to the sword, it hangs over them always, their arbiter and ultimate destroyer. Alexander is as surely destroyed by the sword as are those he conquered with it; the assassin as well as his victim. None the less, the illusion has continued to be entertained that even Jesus can be served with the sword, and may even be induced to take it up himself. Many have at different times, like the Crusaders and Cromwell's Ironsides, marched, sword in hand, supposedly to further his Kingdom; and in our own time we have the curious spectacle of clerical *exaltés* advocating acts of violence in Jesus's name, in the expectation that those who take the sword will triumph with the sword if their cause is just. Before being taken away, Jesus rounds on those who have seized him: *Are ye come out, as against a thief with swords and staves? When I was daily with you in the temple, ye stretched forth no hands against me; but this is your hour, and the*

Then Simon Peter having a sword drew it, and smote the high priest's servant, and cut off his right ear.

STONE CARVING

power of darkness. Yet, he goes on, they must not suppose him to be defenceless; if he had cared, he could have called upon his Father to send him more than twelve legions of angels. This, however, would have belied the Scriptures, which decree that he must fall into their hands. So, eschewing all help from on high, and on earth disposing of none, he submits himself to them, to do with him what they will.

Having thus disposed of violence, power's right arm and chief instrument, Jesus has to confront another of the world's great fantasies – justice. He is called upon to appear before, successively, the Jewish authorities in the person of the High Priest, Caiaphas, and the Sanhedrin; the Roman authorities in the person of the Governor, or Procurator, Pontius Pilate; and, as a Galilean, before the Roman satrap, King Herod. In all the great recorded trials of history, whether Socrates', Jesus's or Nuremberg, the theme, and, in essentials, even the scene, are identical. It would be possible to have one set for the presentation of them all, and simply change the accused, with all the other characters – judges, policemen, witnesses, defence and prosecuting counsel, above all the public – remaining the same. In each case, the strong are condemning the weak, the victor the vanquished, and, with varying degrees of subtlety and sophistication, disguising this as a system of law. To call for justice in this world (which Jesus never once did; nor did he at any point give any indication of expecting justice, or, in any of his reported utterances, so much as mention the word) amounts in practice to calling for something which by its nature cannot be just – viz. law. To cry out for justice in human terms is as foolish as calling for iced water in the middle of the Sahara. From men we can look for mercy and pity, and, thanks to Jesus, from God for forgiveness; but Justice – never! How delicately Pascal makes the same point when he says that judges have to wear wigs and ermine and red robes! Otherwise, who would take seriously their fraudulent judgments? If we were capable of rendering or receiving justice we should need no laws to codify injustice; no parliamentarians to make laws, lawyers to argue them, police to enforce them, revolutionaries to reject them with a view to remaking them in due course, prisons and executioners to dispose of all who refuse to abide by them. 'I only care for justice', is the cry of every counterfeiter, whether of the hopes, the fears, or just the cash, wherewith we live. By comparison with asking for justice, the moon is a trifle, eternity a throwaway line, and happiness on ready sale at every supermarket.

Jesus's first appearance is before the Sanhedrin presided over by Caiaphas, to whose house Jesus is taken from the Garden of Gethsemane. On his way there, a curious episode is reported in St Mark's

Gospel. A young man followed behind Jesus with particular intensity. He was clothed only in a linen cloth, perhaps because, hearing the uproar, he had risen hurriedly from bed. Or perhaps he was another deranged person drawn to Jesus, like the man in the country of the Gadarenes. His eagerness in following Jesus aroused suspicion, and a move was made to take him also into custody; whereupon he broke away, naked, into the night, having left his linen cloth with those who had laid hands on him. Who was he? Some have suggested St Mark himself. I think myself that he must have been a reporter on the then equivalent of the *Jerusalem Post*, out looking for a story. Caiaphas and the Sanhedrin really hate Jesus. In their eyes, he is not just a malefactor and con-man who has acquired a following by wild talk and bogus miracles – another and more reprehensible John the Baptist. Much worse than that, he has intruded upon their preserves – the prophecies, claiming to be the Messiah whose coming they foretell. This nondescript, illiterate nobody from, of all places, Nazareth, putting himself forward as the promised Servant of God, the Saviour upon whom all their hopes are centred of seeing the restoration of Israel's fortunes and greatness as God's Chosen People! It is intolerable.

The proceedings begin quietly enough. Various suborned witnesses are produced who quote things Jesus has said which can be twisted into supporting the case against him; notably, the remark about his being able to destroy the Temple and rebuild it in three days. Jesus makes no comment; like Dostoevsky's returned Christ before the Grand Inquisitor, he maintains a complete silence, as though the words poured out in his presence have nothing whatever to do with him. It is the perfect response, and enrages Caiaphas, as it did the Grand Inquisitor. The strength of law and the fraudulent justice it purports to embody, derives from the ease with which we can be involved and entangled in its processes. Just to answer a question is to accept its terms of reference, and so to stand condemned. Caiaphas, enraged by the way Jesus's silence is nullifying the case against him, now steps down from his judicial dais, and, approaching Jesus, asks him why he does not answer his accusers. Still Jesus remains silent. Then Caiaphas loses his head and bawls out: *I adjure thee by the living God, that thou tell us whether thou be the Christ, the Son of God.* At last Jesus speaks: *Thou hast said.* Then he adds: *Hereafter shall ye see the Son of man sitting on the right hand of power, and coming in the clouds of heaven.* It is more than Caiaphas can stand; in his fury he tears at his clothes, and denounces Jesus for speaking blasphemy. Appealing to the other members of the Sanhedrin present, he asks for their opinion, and with one accord they say Jesus deserves to die. Having thus established his guilt and delivered the death sentence, they turn upon Jesus to molest and spit and jeer at him, calling upon him ironically to prophesy as a Messiah should.

Was Jesus guilty? Of course he was. Just as Joan of Arc was guilty, and Sir Thomas More, and Servetus; just as all the Old Bolsheviks tried by Stalin were guilty, and all the vanquished Nazis tried at Nuremberg by their vanquishers were guilty. Van der Lubbe, Eichmann, Cardinal Mindszenty, Robert Oppenheimer, Pétain and many, many others, all guilty. The hero of Kafka's novel, *The Trial*, has no clear idea what he is accused of, or why. All he knows is that he is guilty, of the only crime there is, the essence of all criminality at all times and in all circumstances – being on the losing side. Jesus, with his divine perceptiveness, accepts this situation, only occasionally lapsing by pointing out that, if he cared but to say the word, there were legions of angels who would spring to his defence and deliver him at once from paltry enemies like Caiaphas. If, in fact, he had summoned them, it would at a stroke have established his innocence; Caiaphas would have at once withdrawn all his charges, Pilate have put his name in for a minor decoration, and Herod have offered him a lucrative post at his Court. Instead, Jesus stuck fast to his guilt. Jesus's guilt is our innocence; as his captivity is our freedom, and his death our life.

Having established Jesus's guilt, and decided that it deserved the death penalty, according to the Gospels it was obligatory for the Sanhedrin to get the sentence approved by the Roman authorities and executed by them. If the Sanhedrin had been authorized to carry out the death penalty on its own account, then presumably, Jesus would have been stoned like Stephen instead of crucified. In that case there would have been no Cross; and so no occasion for God to transform a barbaric instrument for putting a man to death into a symbol of the salvation of all mankind. It was not just that Jesus had to be put to death; he had to be crucified. The appearance before Pilate was in a quite different vein from the one before the Sanhedrin, and Jesus himself reacted differently. In Pilate's eyes, Jesus was not the hateful and dangerous figure the Sanhedrin saw in him, but just another element in the endless turbulence of Judaea, for whose law and order, as Procurator, Pilate was responsible. The only point at which Roman, as distinct from Jewish, interests were directly involved arose out of Jesus's alleged claim to be the King of the Jews. This sounded like subversion in Roman terms, and if it got to the Emperor's ears, maybe in a garbled form, might easily make

And some began to spit on him, and to cover his face, and to buffet him, and to say unto him, Prophesy: and the servants did strike him with the palms of their hands.

PAINTING BY GRÜNEWALD

trouble for Pilate, and set back his career in the Colonial Service. At the same time, Jesus clearly intrigued Pilate, and there is even a suggestion that his wife was attracted by Jesus's teaching, and had some sort of dream which led her to warn her husband against being a party to Jesus's Crucifixion. Her name – Claudia Procula – occurs among the authorized list of saints in the Greek Orthodox Church.

It was, in any case, a curious confrontation – the cultivated, sophisticated Roman facing the unlettered Jewish mystic; the man of the world facing the man out of this world; Caesar's representative in Judaea facing God's representative on earth. It would be attractive in a way to suppose that Jesus made an indelible impression on Pilate, but more likely Anatole France's judgment is correct in his story about someone who sought out Pilate in old age to get his impressions of Jesus, only to find that he did not remember him at all. There were many such religious fanatics of one sort and another knocking about in Judaea in Pilate's time there. He is more likely to have remembered John the Baptist, if only because of Herod's involvement; the story about Salome's dance, and her request for the Baptist's head on a charger, will certainly have gone the rounds in the sort of society Pilate frequented. In the same sort of way, in the days of the Raj a Governor of Bombay might easily forget the case of a young lawyer named Gandhi, lately returned from South Africa, who had got mixed up in subversive activities.

The dialogue between Pilate and Jesus is one of the key conversations in the Gospels – like the one with Nicodemus, or with the rich ruler, or with Martha of Bethany. Jesus could speak with Pilate, as he could not with Caiaphas, because Pilate was genuinely seeking elucidation, whereas Caiaphas's only purpose was to formulate Jesus's guilt, upon which he had already decided in his own mind. Pilate begins by asking Jesus if he really is the King of the Jews; to which Jesus replies with another question: Is Pilate asking him this on his own account? Or have others put it into his head that he has claimed to be King of the Jews? Pilate evades answering so specific a question with a rhetorical one: *Am I a Jew?* Jesus, he goes on, has been handed over to him by his fellow countrymen, notably, the High Priest and the Sanhedrin. They must have some reason for it, which brings him to the heart of the matter: *What hast thou done?* Jesus answers in the unforgettable and truly sublime words: *My Kingdom is not of this world.* If his Kingdom were of this world, he tells Pilate, his followers would be up in arms to save him from being handed over to the Jewish authorities. (One thinks of the scared disciples and their two swords!) As things are, his authority derives from other than earthly sources. This seems to Pilate to imply a kingly role of sorts. *Art thou a king then?*, he asks. You say I'm a king, Jesus replies, but I'll tell you what I am – and then comes the stupendous answer: *To this end was I born, and for this cause came I into the world, that I should bear witness unto the truth. Every one that is of the truth heareth my voice.*

Poor Pilate was overwhelmed, and could only feebly mutter: *What is truth?* – three words for which he will be known to the end of time. Even if Pilate had seriously sought an answer to his question, Jesus would only have told him, as he did the disciples, that he, the Son of Man was *the way, the truth, and the life.* It was something they dimly understood, but that Pilate would not have understood at all. By virtue of his office, he was perforce concerned with justice, with law and order and government, rather than with truth. To escape from any further involvement, he hurried out to the Sanhedrin men who had brought Jesus to him, they having remained outside for fear of contaminating themselves for the Passover. Pilate told them that he could find no fault in Jesus, but they were the more insistent he should be crucified, saying: *He stirreth up the people, teaching throughout all Jewry, beginning from Galilee to this place.* Civil servants are always on the look out for some means to extricate themselves from having to take decisions; for anything which will enable them to scrawl across a file: Refer to such a department, or to this or that person, thereby ensuring its dispatch elsewhere. Pilate saw such a floating spar in the word 'Galilee', and grasped it like a drowning man. Was Jesus a Galilean, then? Yes, he was. In that case, he came within Herod's jurisdiction, and should be sent to him forthwith.

Herod, like Pilate – who normally resided in Caesarea – was in Jeruslem for the Passover. Usually, when he came to Jerusalem, Pilate stayed in Herod's magnificent palace on Mount Sion, but as Herod was there he occupied the fortress Antonio, conveniently overlooking the Temple, and a secure citadel in case of rioting, which was always liable to break out in Jerusalem during Jewish festivals. It was to Herod's palace that Jesus was taken, and there brought into the presence of the princeling to whom he had once referred as *that fox.* Herod had for long been curious about Jesus, and wanted to see him, but Jesus, remembering the fate of John the Baptist, kept well out of his way, sometimes dodging about on the Lake of Galilee to avoid coming under his jurisdiction. Herod, no doubt, hoped that Jesus might be induced to perform one of his miracles to entertain his Court. Though Herod fired questions at him, and the Jews who had entered the palace with him went on vehemently shouting accusations at him, Jesus kept silent, this time, one assumes, out of contempt. It is interesting to reflect that if Jesus had consented to join the Zealots and take a leading part in the Jewish nationalist movement, it would have been with a view to transferring sovereignty in Judaea from Roman hands to some indigenous monarch like Herod; comparable to transferring sovereignty from a gilt-coated Excellency to a Kaunda or Kenyatta or Amin. Such a transference would scarcely have needed an Incarnation to bring it about. Unable to get any response or entertaining miracle out of Jesus, Herod with his soldiers *set him at nought, and mocked him, and arrayed him in a gorgeous robe, and sent him back to Pilate.* For some unexplained reason, this liaison between the satrap and the Procurator over Jesus led to a more friendly relationship between them than had subsisted heretofore. Perhaps an unconscious awareness of having seen God in person, and of having equally failed to respond adequately, drew them together.

With Jesus back on his hands, Pilate again tries to save him; offering to chastise him and then release him on the ground that both he and Herod have found he has done nothing deserving of the death penalty. However, the mob which is now at Jesus's heels, and will stay with him till he dies, shouts implacably: *Crucify him! Crucify him!* Such mobs are a constant element in history, and are easily manipulated – in this case, by the Sanhedrin. They can be as readily induced to shout for the death of a martyr as for the glorification of a tyrant, and, harnessed to a consensus, can easily seem to speak for everyone. A contemporary version is the studio audience. To see the floor-manager at work warming one up, to be ready to cheer or laugh or groan or hiss as and when required, is to be at the very heart of the contemporary power process. The procedure is applicable to all systems of government, democratic, oligarchic, authoritarian, paternalistic, hierarchical or monarchical. Pilate now remembers that it is the custom at Passover time to grant a pardon to some prisoner designated by the Sanhedrin, and suggests that Jesus should be the beneficiary on this occasion. Again the mob frustrates his purpose, yelling for Barabbas, not Jesus, to be released; he by all accounts being a sort of Che Guevara of the time, a guerrilla leader or freedom-fighter, who *for a certain sedition made in the city, and for murder, was cast into prison.* Thus Jesus's fate is sealed. Pilate's ironical question: *Shall I crucify your king?*, only enrages the Sanhedrin the more, and the chief priests respond with undertones of menace from Pilate's point of view: *We have no King but Caesar.* Having ceremonially washed his hands to signify that he is *innocent of the blood of this just person*, on his orders

They cried, saying, Crucify him, crucify him.

PAINTING BY BOSCH

Barabbas is released and Jesus delivered to his executioners. If, contrariwise, Jesus had been released and Barabbas crucified, it is extremely improbable that Barabbianity would have swept over the Western World as Christianity did. Of the subsequent fate of Barabbas we know nothing, but we may imagine him continuing with his subversive activities; perhaps joining the Qumran Community, and there hearing vaguely of the spread of Christianity, whose founder was the crazy King of the Jews Pilate had suggested releasing in his place.

Pilate's numerous references to Jesus as King of the Jews were, of course, deliberately intended to infuriate the Sanhedrin – which they succeeded in doing. They also, perhaps, helped Pilate to get over whatever qualms he had about sending someone in whom he could find no fault to be crucified. After all, in so far as Jesus had, however absurdly in Pilate's terms, claimed to be King of the Jews, he was guilty of subversion, whose punishment by Roman Law was crucifixion. It was to rub in this point that Pilate had a board prepared, to be put over Jesus's head when he was on the Cross, announcing in the three languages to be heard among the literate in Jerusalem – Hebrew, Latin and Greek – that he was King of the Jews. Naturally, the Sanhedrin objected, but Pilate, on this issue at least, was adamant, and refused to amend the inscription to read that Jesus *claimed* to be King of the Jews. *What I have written I have written*, he said. So, as Pilate wished, Jesus died under a notice identifying him as King of the Jews. Jesus himself spoke Aramaic, the local vernacular, and will have been unable to read the notice anyway. In the event, the joke, such as it was, misfired. Jesus proved to be King of the Jews in a sense infinitely transcending anything that Pilate could ever have imagined. At the same time, the mockery in Pilate's inscription redounded, not to Jesus's discredit, but to that of all kings, then and thereafter. For those with eyes to see, there never would be a wholly serious king again.

Likewise, the buffoonery of the Roman soldiers when they dressed Jesus up in a scarlet robe, and plaited a crown of thorns and put it on his head, and gave him a reed to hold in his right hand like a sceptre; then knelt down before him and mocked him, saying with ribald reverence: *Hail, King of the Jews!* They, too, were not, as they supposed, just ridiculing a poor deluded man about to die, but holding up to ridicule all kings, all rulers, all exercisers of authority who ever had been or were to be. They were making power itself derisory; ensuring that thenceforth under every crown there would be thorns, and under every scarlet robe, stricken flesh.

In the Garden of Gethsemane Jesus had shown up the fantasy of violence; then, when he appeared successively before the Sanhedrin, Pilate and Herod, the fantasy of justice. Now, in this dreadful masquerade of himself as a ribald King of the Jews, the fantasy of power itself is exposed for ever. There were, of course, tyrants who would rise up after Jesus's death in his name; and before very long a Pontiff would be crowned in Rome with a triple crown as Jesus's representative on earth. Yet there was always to be, thanks to Jesus, a reservation as to whether the potentate in question might not, like Pilate's King of the Jews, be a figure of farce rather than of awe. Behind the songs of praise, however loud, and the adulatory speeches, however fulsome, the sound of mocking laughter would always be heard. However absolute the authority – divine right of kings, infallible Popes, Holy Roman and other emperors – Jesus's presence at some point would make itself felt, raising the question: Is that jewelled crown plaited thorns? That red robe drag? That gleaming sceptre a mere reed? Those fawning courtiers jeering soldiers?

The anointed monarch has to bow down at the altar rails before another and greater king. In the mystery of the Passion the world's judgments are turned upside-down, so that what seems strongest is most weak, what seems most serious, most farcical, what seems most imposing, most derisory. Outside the mystery of the Passion, however, power becomes all embracing, with nothing to moderate its demands or mitigate its cruelty; pursued for its own sake alone, as in Orwell's *Nineteen Eighty-Four*. The unanointed monarchs of our time, the Stalins and the Hitlers and the Mao Tse-tungs, have proved infinitely more tyrannous than ever the anointed ones were. If, as often seems to be the case, we have driven Jesus away, or at any rate back to the catacombs, then we are totally at the mercy of our rulers, whoever they may be and whatever the ideology on behalf of which they purport to govern. The only antidote to the poison from Caesar's laurel crown comes from Jesus's crown of thorns. He alone can deliver us from the monstrosities and buffooneries of power, as has been discovered by the most perceptive spirits of our time, such as Solzhenitsyn. Faced with power at its most unbridled and most brutal, they turn for help and comfort, not to Universal Declarations of Human Rights and other pronouncements, solemn undertakings, Covenants and Charters in a similar vein, but to the man wearing a crown of thorns, decked out in a red robe of absurdity and with a court of jeering soldiers. There alone the sting of power is drawn and its pretensions are exploded, and the princes of this world have no recourse but, like Judas, to flee into the night.

Having disposed of violence, justice and power, three horseman of the Apocalypse, there was a fourth to be unseated – death. This had to be done by dying himself, in the most agonizing and ignominious way, thereby demonstrating that death was not an ending but a renewal of life; as a grain of wheat planted in the ground dies in order to sprout and become, first a green shoot, then a golden ear. As the Apostle Paul was to put it in his incomparable Letter to the Corinthians: *When this corruptible shall have put on incorruption, and this mortal shall have put on immortality, then shall be brought to pass the saying that is written: Death is swallowed up in victory.* Jesus on the Cross is the promise of that victory, as the Resurrection is its realization.

As power without the intervention of Jesus tends to become absolute and tyrannous, so death without his intervention opens up the ghastly prospect of our mortal lives continuing for ever; in the manner of the Struldbrugs Gulliver encountered on his third voyage, to Laputa. These unfortunates, Gulliver discovered, were fated to be immortal, and presented such a spectacle of wretchedness that, he decides, 'no tyrant could invent a death into which I would not run with pleasure from such a life'. Our own essays in the direction of projecting our lives in this world indefinitely are scarcely more promising. Nor is our conspiracy of silence about death, hoping that somehow, by making it unmentionable, it will disappear. Or our hopes of some magical discovery of a death pill matching the birth pill, the one ensuring that we never die, as the other, a necessary corollary, ensures that we live in a state of inviolate and blissful infertility for ever.

To achieve this last illumination – the abolition of death by dying – Jesus must hump his Cross along the Via Dolorosa leading to the Place of Skulls, the hill Golgotha just outside the city wall. In the little procession accompanying him there are two other miscreants, also to be crucified and carrying their crosses. After his scourging and other ill-treatment Jesus is too weak to bear the weight of his Cross, and a bystander, Simon of Cyrene, is induced to carry it for him. I have always had a special regard for this Simon, whose good fortune it was to be on hand when the Roman soldiers were looking for someone to be pressed into shouldering Jesus's Cross. I feel that, though I should certainly have failed in every respect to be a worthy follower of Jesus, outdoing Peter in denying him, Thomas in doubting him, and perhaps even Judas in betraying him, I might just have been up to doing what Simon did. Some women trailing along behind Jesus, and noting his wretched state, begin to bewail and lament; whereupon he turns to them and tells them not to weep for him but for themselves and for their children in view of the tragic days which are surely coming, when it will seem as though the barren are blessed, and people will cry out in their terror for the mountains to fall upon them and for the hills to cover them. *For if they do these things in a green tree*, he asks, *what shall be done in the dry?* Forty years later, when the Romans destroyed Jerusalem, if any of the women were still alive, they would have cause to remember Jesus's words. Today, twenty centuries later, we have cause to remember them yet again.

For Christians the Via Dolorosa has provided an image of the way of redemption, as its Stations of the Cross, portrayed by one means or another in churches and cathedrals, have played a notable part in Christian worship. Nowadays, the image is unacceptable. A man stumbling along, bearing on his back the frame on to which he will be stretched and nailed, as we in our flesh bear the urges which stretch and pinion us – this will not do at all. Better than the Via Dolorosa, the motorway, six lanes a side, with cars interminably processing from nowhere to nowhere; sounds and sweet airs coming from the car radio, as also news of murder and sudden death, which, along with his drooping cigarette, keep the driver in a suitable mood of somnolence and vacuity, so that soothed and bewitched by the everlasting movement, he feels he is going on, on, for ever, till the end of time, with new vistas of tarmac endlessly unfolding. Or, better still, a conveyor belt, a moving cornucopia which shapes and bears abundance to an avid world. Or, best of all perhaps, the evolutionary climb, from primeval mud to twentieth-century man in all his glory, able to go to the moon, travel faster than light, whose very genes are counted and whose organs are replaceable, who can fornicate without procreating, and eat without fattening, and flash a gleaming smile without being happy. Better almost anything than the stumbling jeered-at figure on his way to Golgotha and death.

Now we come to the climax of the story of Jesus, the point to which everything has been leading – his death on the Cross. In a sense, it is true of every life that death is its culmination; if we did not die there would be no point in living. With Jesus's death, the world began again; even to the trivial point that happenings in our Western calendar are dated in relation to it – BC or AD. According to the Gospels, Jesus's death was accompanied by various supernatural happenings; as, the earth did quake, darkness covered the land, and the veil of the Temple was rent in twain from top to bottom. Records of the time, it appears, in so far as they exist, do not point to anything unusual in the rising and the setting of the sun at the time, nor to the incidence of an exceptional

It was the third hour,
and they crucified him.

DETAIL OF PAINTING
BY JAN VAN EYCK

earthquake. It may equally be doubted whether, if television cameras had happened to be set up at the entrance to the tomb in which Jesus was laid, they would have recorded the removal of the stone which sealed the tomb, or the emergence from it of the risen Jesus. If they had, then the sublime drama of Jesus's death and resurrection would have been reduced to the dimensions of what is euphemistically called a 'real life documentary' – a contradiction in terms if ever there was one. A surgeon can legitimately claim that, in foraging about in a patient's inside, he found no trace of a soul, or an astronaut that, riding through the stratosphere, he caught no glimpse of pearly gates; but if the surgeon did stumble on a soul lurking among our entrails, or the astronaut did pick up intimations of a celestial city on his radar screen, it would prove conclusively that there are no souls and there is no Heaven. Eternity disappears if Time can comprehend it, and God has no existence if Man can see and know Him, other than through the mercy of Jesus Christ. In any case, the alleged supernatural accompaniments of Jesus's death matter little, compared with the stupendous reality of his death and its actual consequences.

The grisly arrangements are made for disposing of Jesus's body on his Cross and hoisting it up; similarly with the two malefactors, one on either side of him. As was the custom, Jesus is to be crucified naked, his clothes being divided among the soldiers – one of their perks; in this particular case, meagre enough. The main garment cannot be divided, and so they play dice for it, thereby fulfilling a prophecy: *They part my garments among them, and cast lots upon my vesture.* Jesus refuses to swallow the drugged drink normally provided as an act of compassion to those about to be crucified, he has to be aware of his suffering. His supreme sacrifice, to be valid, must be conscious. The crowd gathered round the three crosses include soldiers, one or two Sanhedrin representatives to ensure that everything goes according to plan, spectators with a sick taste for viewing such happenings, the mob, and a little group of women who love Jesus, including Mary, his mother, and Mary Magdalene. The only disciple mentioned as being present is John, to whom Jesus entrusts the care of his mother – *Behold thy mother! Woman, behold thy son!* There is a lot of jeering – this miraculous healer cured others, but cannot cure himself; this braggart, who boasted he could destroy the Temple and rebuild it in three days, does not seem to be able to come down from his Cross; this *soi-disant* King of the Jews says he trusts in God, then let God *deliver him now, if he will have him: for he said, I am the Son of God.* Even one of the malefactors joins in the jeering, asking why, if Jesus is, as he claims, the Son of God, he does not arrange for all three of them to be saved. The other rebukes him, pointing out that, unlike them, Jesus has committed no crime. For this Jesus promises him that they will be together that very day in Paradise.

It is now that Jesus's despair breaks from him in the opening words of Psalm 22: *My God, my God, why hast thou forsaken me?* At this dark moment when death is so near, and Jesus is utterly alone and at the mercy of his enemies, he feels himself to be separated even from God. Whatever vague hopes he may have had in his mortal being that somehow God would intervene on his behalf must be abandoned. God, it seems, has deserted him; the sacrifice he is required to make is to face death *as a man*, with no legions of angels ready at a moment's notice to come and save him, no heavenly throne awaiting him, no clouds of glory for him to ride in on and disconcert his enemies. Most terrible of all, with no loving God to be concerned about him; whose particular Son he is, and on whose behalf he is nailed to a cross and shortly to die. At this point a physical need intrudes itself, and he cries out: *I thirst* – the two words Mother Teresa has had inscribed on the altars of all the houses of the Missionaries of Charity. Some bystanders taking pity on his plight, and seeing a vessel full of vinegar to hand, put a sponge full of the vinegar *upon hyssop, and put it to his mouth.* Having received the vinegar, Jesus says: *It is finished*; then bows his head, and gives up his spirit.

Thus, in earthly terms, ends the story of Jesus. Actually, far from ending, it is only the beginning. St Paul, a persecutor of Christians, will become Jesus's most ardent and effective advocate, and spread the good news of the coming of the Kingdom to Europe, where it will provide the basis for a new great civilization to rise up on the ruins of Rome, and thence come to be heard, as Jesus required, in every corner of the world. More than that, Jesus himself, though he has died, will live on in the world; not just through his followers and his teaching as other great spirits have, but *as a person*. Socrates was a wise and noble man, but no one has found in him posthumously a day-to-day friend and companion on whose behalf lives of outstanding love and dedication have been lived. The saints have sojourned among us, and left behind them blessed memories and continuing inspiration, but they have gone from our midst when their time came. Similarly great artists have bequeathed to us their works, but they, too, in due course have departed, never to return. What is unique about Jesus is that, on the testimony and in the experience of innumerable people, of all sorts and conditions, of all races and nationalities, from the simplest and most primitive to the most sophisticated and cultivated, he remains alive.

Joseph . . . went unto Pilate, and begged the body of Jesus. And he took it down.

STONE CARVING

The first manifestation of Jesus's presence in the world came immediately after his death. Thanks to one of his rich secret followers, Joseph of Arimathea, a new tomb hollowed out of a rock was available for Jesus's body, and permission was given for him to be laid in it. With the help of another of his wealthy followers, Nicodemus, the body was hurriedly embalmed and swathed in linen bands. A large stone was placed in position to close the mouth of the tomb, and guards posted to ensure that no attempt was made to remove the body in order to claim that, as he had prophesied, Jesus had risen from the dead. None the less, when at midnight the following day three women came to the tomb, they found the stone rolled away and Jesus's body removed. Thereafter Jesus appeared on numerous occasions, in his bodily shape and with his bodily needs.

There has been much heated controversy, running to millions of words, about the Resurrection. As, for instance, how the stone sealing the tomb came to be removed, why the soldiers guarding the tomb apparently noticed nothing. A notion came to me once when I was in the Holy Land that maybe some body-snatcher heard in his dim-witted way in Jerusalem that the King of the Jews was up for execution. So he rushes to Golgotha on the look-out for pickings; waits till the job is done, finds out where the corpse has been laid, drags the stone away, and then, when no one is watching, decamps with the body. What a disappointment! This King of the Jews has no crown, no jewels, no orbs, no sceptre, no ring. There is just a worthless, broken, naked body, which the man abandons in disgust to the vultures; and they, in their turn, leave the bones to whiten in the desert sun. Precious, precious bones!

When we think of friends who have died we see them as we knew them – as mortal beings, with mortal needs and habiliments – even though we are well aware that, if we believe they have entered upon a new mode of existence, they will have undergone a total trans-formation. In the same way, when Shakespeare introduces Banquo's ghost in the body and lineaments of Banquo the man, this is not because he supposes him to have been unchanged by his death, but because it is the only way the audience can be induced to recognize him. Similarly, when the disciples were conscious of Jesus's presence among them after the Crucifixion they saw him as they had known him; in a body, wearing clothes, speaking and eating. At the same time, it was his presence among them, not what they seemed to see and hear and touch in him, which prepared them to receive the Holy Spirit, and undertake their great task of founding and propagating the Christian religion. Following them, subsequent generations of

187

Christians, up to the present time, have likewise been conscious of Jesus's presence among them, and of the transformation it wrought in their lives; the joy and lovingness and enhanced perceptiveness it brought them in this world where Jesus lived and taught and died, and the vista it opened up of his Kingdom which is not of this world.

Did Jesus rise from the dead in the sense of resuming his mortal existence? Was he the same man after the Resurrection as he had been before he was crucified, except that his body showed the marks of the nails that had been driven into his hands and feet, and the hole in his side where the Roman soldier's sword had pierced him to make sure that he was well and truly dead? It was these wounds which the Apostle Thomas insisted he must touch before he could bring himself to believe that the Resurrection had really happened – *Except I shall see in his hands the print of the nails, and put my finger into the print of the nails, and thrust my hand into his side, I will not believe.*

Eight days later, when the risen Jesus is with his disciples, having suddenly appeared among them even though the doors of the room they are in remained shut, he says to Thomas: *Thomas, reach hither thy finger, and behold my hands; and reach hither thy hand, and thrust it into my side: and be not faithless but believing.* To which Thomas, having followed Jesus's instructions, can only reply: *My Lord and my God.* Jesus thereupon draws a distinction between those who, like Thomas, believe because they see and touch, and those – more blessed – who have neither seen nor touched, and yet believe.

Since Thomas's time there have been innumerable Christians who have believed without seeing. Today even those who see find difficulty in believing; and the prevailing view is that, in so far as the Resurrection can be said to have happened at all, it signified no more than the continuing influence Jesus was to have on the lives and thoughts and hopes of his followers. At best it is seen as providing a happy ending to a sad tale, whose hero, having fallen into the hands of his enemies and been done to death by them, unexpectedly reappears, hale and hearty, like Sherlock Holmes turning up again after Conan Doyle had disposed of him finally in a previous story.

It may be doubted whether such a dénouement as this would have given rise to all the acclamation on Easter Sunday through the centuries. Tolstoy has described how Russian peasants used to greet one another joyously at Easter-time with 'Christ is risen!', as though this momentous event had only just happened. Throughout Christendom the occasion has been one for thankfulness and rejoicing, beautifully expressed by Psalm 95, the *Venite: O come, let us sing*

unto the Lord: let us make a joyful noise to the rock of our salvation.
Co-incidentally with the promise of spring, the yearly renewal of
crops and flowers and the songs of birds, comes this other Resurrection, with its promise of a spiritual rebirth for all who seek it. The
Risen Christ is the image of Fallen Man redeemed; of his ultimate,
and only enduring, liberation; of the freedom he has sought so
ardently, so valiantly and so vainly at hustings and on battlefields, in
disputes and in debates, and in the secret strivings of rebellious
minds, now at last attained.

As we have seen, to fulfil the purpose of the Incarnation Jesus had
to be both Man and God; only so could God make Himself known
to men, and men truly relate themselves to God. On the Cross Jesus
died as Man, but only to rise from the dead as God. This was the
Resurrection. Once again it is not a question of either-or; the
Crucifixion did not leave Jesus dead *or* alive, but dead *and* alive. The
human tragedy of his death was swallowed up in the beatific vision of
deathlessness which the Resurrection accorded to his disciples, and
after them to all who loved and followed him. If he had come down
from the Cross as his tormentors called on him to do, it could only
have been as Man, with another death before him; like Lazarus, who
was raised from the dead to live on as a man, until such time as he
definitively died. Jesus, when he was crucified, died irretrievably as
Man, and in rising from the dead entered upon his inheritance of
everlasting life. It was the Incarnation in reverse; God Incarnate was
Jesus, and Jesus Resurrected was God. *I am the resurrection, and the
life,* Jesus had said to Martha of Bethany when about to raise her
brother from the dead. In showing himself to his disciples after his
body had been embalmed and his tomb sealed, the truth of these
words was made manifest for ever.

When he was on the Cross before he died, speaking as a man, Jesus
promised one of the miscreants crucified beside him that they would
dine together in Paradise that very night. On the other hand, after he
has died, and speaking as the Risen Christ, he tells Mary Magdalene:
Touch me not; for I am not yet ascended to my Father. In other words, he
has ceased to be flesh, but is not yet one with God. The same point is
made when the angels in Jesus's empty tomb are reported as asking the
women who have come to embalm him: *Why seek ye the living among
the dead?* The tomb is for the dead, they are saying, but Jesus is alive
and so not to be found there. The angels go on to remind the women of
how Jesus had told them in Galilee that *the Son of man must be delivered
into the hands of sinful men, and be crucified, and the third day rise again.*
So why should they be surprised?

Later, to correct the impression that the Risen Jesus was just a disembodied spirit briefly haunting the earth and soon to disappear into Heaven, the Gospels go out of their way to stress his physical necessities. Thus, on one occasion he asks the disciples for food: *Have ye here any meat?*, and they give him *a piece of broiled fish, and a honeycomb*. Again, at Tiberias, when the disciples have been fishing all through the night but have caught nothing, at dawn they see someone standing on the nearby shore who tells them: *Cast the net on the right side of the ship, and ye shall find*. This they do and are not able to draw in the net for the multitude of fishes. It is John who recognizes the stranger who has brought them this fantastic catch as Jesus. *It is the Lord*, he exclaims, and Peter impulsively jumps into the water to swim to him. When they come in with their great haul they see *a fire of coals there, and fish laid thereon, and bread*, and Jesus dispenses this food to them as he did to the five thousand. Yet again, to endow his disciples with the Holy Spirit he physically breathes on them. During his ministry, he touched the tongues of the dumb to make them speak and the eyes of the blind to make them see, and now his breath gives the disciples the strength, the courage and the words to undertake the stupendous task entrusted to them – to go *into all the world and preach the gospel to every creature*.

Thomas was fortunate; he could see and touch the Crucifixion wounds, his fingers guided thereto by Jesus himself. Subsequent Thomases have had to probe and grope with mere questioning. How could Jesus eat when his body had been drained of its blood? What sort of digestive system did he have? What clothes was he wearing, and who had provided them, when his own had been taken by the Roman soldiers, and his shroud was found in the empty tomb? To put such questions is to miss the essential point, grasped at once by Tolstoy's peasants with their 'Christ is risen!' The Resurrection is not just something that happened; it goes on happening as spring goes on coming. It is the indestructible hope that has sustained Christians through the harlequinade of history. If Jesus did not rise from the dead, St Paul tells the Christians in Corinth, and in this world only we have hope in Christ, *then is our preaching vain*, and *we are of all men most miserable*. Without the triumph over death that the Resurrection represents, he is saying, Jesus's Kingdom is as illusory as all the others – as Caesar's, as the Dictatorship of the Proletariat that can never be overthrown, as Hitler's Reich that is to last for a thousand years. If there was no Resurrection, then Jesus really was forsaken on the Cross, and his ministry a fiasco. With his last gasp of mortal breath he said: *It is finished*, and there the story would have ended, except that with his immortal breath he added: *Lo, I am with you alway, even unto the end of the world.*

In earthly terms, death is the only certainty. All my mortal mind can know for sure is that this hand, writing these words, will falter and become inert, and the intelligence choosing and arranging them become inoperative. Flesh and intelligence equally doomed shortly to extinction after so brief and fleeting an existence – no more than a dragonfly's, with its bright wings and exquisitely precise movements darting about in the sun. As the psalmist says, *We spend our years as a tale that is told . . .* and are *soon cut off, and we fly away.* This strange, inescapable fate is common to every living creature, from a bacillus to Michelangelo; the tale varies but the outcome is the same. Confronted with it, we may rage, despair, induce forgetfulness, solace ourselves with fantasies that science will in due course discover how we came to be here and to what end, and how we may project our existence, individually or collectively, into some Brave New World spanning the universe in which Man reigns supreme. God's alternative proposition is the Resurrection – a man dying who rises from the dead. Like Pascal with his famous wager, I close with the offer and say: 'Done!', joining in the joyous shout that has echoed through the Christian centuries: 'Christ is risen!'

That the Resurrection happened, and that in consequence of it Jesus's followers who had scattered drew together again, resolved to go about their Master's business, seems to me indubitably true. Likewise, Jesus's claim to be the Light of the World, and his related promise that through him we may be reborn into new men, liberated from servitude to the ego and our appetites into the glorious liberty of the children of God. Compared with these tremendous certainties, dubieties about the precise circumstances of Jesus's birth, ministry, death on the Cross and continuing presence in the world, seem sterile and unprofitable. Either Jesus never was or he still is. As a typical product of these confused times, with a sceptical mind and a sensual disposition, diffidently and unworthily, but with the utmost certainty, I assert that he still is. If the story of Jesus had ended on Golgotha, it would indeed be of a Man Who Died, but as two thousand years later the Man's promise that *where two or three are gathered together in my name, there am I in the midst of them,* manifestly still holds, it is actually the story of a Man Who Lives.

Acknowledgments for illustrations